What people are saying about Human.

In this book Matthew offers courageous authenticity and vulnerability. With wonder and curiosity he opens the living letter of his heart and invites us to find ourselves in his story. Poet, philosopher and pilgrim, Matthew is a trustworthy guide.

~ *Jill Weber, 24/7 Prayer*

John Foreman wrote about a new way to be human. Matthew reminds us that being human isn't new, its ancient. An invitation to get honest, that is as much philosophical as it is theological. Presented with compelling vision, it will both provoke and inspire you - as it did for me.

~ *Jon Cilliers, Anthem Church*

Matthew's writing is raw, real and charming. His poetic style explores the deeper questions of life in a way that provokes the imagination and captures your attention. If you are wrestling with meaning and ready for a journey, this book is well worth your time.

~ *Madz Deyzel, Edify*

Through refreshing vulnerability and honest reflection, Matthew invites us to pause and listen beneath the surface of our lives to those deep longings that call us to be human. Reading this book was a visceral experience that caused me to wander down paths of healing and joy. May it do the same for you.

~ *Xavier Moran, Follower*

Matthew Lewis

HUMAN

How our deepest longings lead us home.

SEED

Human: How our deepest longings lead us home

First published in South Africa in 2024 by Matthew Lewis

Published in association with SEED

(A ministry of Conduit Ministries NPC 2019/084914/08)

Published in association with Groep7 Drukkers en Uitgewers (Pty) Ltd

Trade Paperback ISBN: 978-0-6398322-1-0

Cover design and typesetting by Jeremy Miller, www.tallandstout.co.za

Illustrations by Tenille Douglas, @tenille_art on Instagram.

To those in search of a stream

I saw a dead man walking.
Dragging thick tracks through worn dirt in search of a stream.
He hobbled past in blaze of day, head bent away from a billboard.
It was meant to guide him, but the words fell silent.

"Fresh water here!"

Those triggers cut violent in a mind that would rather risk confinement
than crack thin the door to let lies in.
He winced with tired eyes and a back full of knives that dripped lies
from the cold pew that morning.
Deaf to my calling, he just kept walking.
Haggard and hauling regret, like a plough in the dirt digging ditches
for faith that dribbled fast past ankles and into a shallow grave.

A dusty cup.
A trembling hand.
Mouth dry as sand, he scanned mirage horizons still searching for a stream.

And then he vanished.

Not quite a dream.
More like a memory.
You see that dead man walking was me.
Lost out in the blazing, hunched over like a half dome.
Straining tight eyes at bleached skies, scanning specks that circled patient over
my fading.

Hope leaked easy in those days.

Salt streams engraving burnt skin with tears that sipped strong as the pain they
were made in.

Scars.

They still linger like landmarks, tracing the faces of strangers and neighbours in the places I call home.
They make loud the storm clouds that even now run rivers down black tar and dirt paths.
Flooding aircon halls and self-drive cars.
Flowing fast through dead-end bars where the desperate dredge bottles for relief.
All in search of a stream.

You see, we're all that dead man walking.

Pride won't let us say it.
We're wrapped up in life hacks and scrolling for filters.
But sometimes, when the door slams and silence settles thick as fog, we slowly sense the rattling.
That ricochet of empty gains now tumbling through the space that used to hold a heartbeat.

If we're brave we let the ache breathe.
We take a knee to set the pain free.
Wait naked in the rain until the sky bleeds mercy.

At least that's where He found me.

That dead man.
Walking.
Except not dead at all.

I felt His pulse like thunder when He dragged me from the floor.
His blazing gaze that warmed my face.
His whisper calmed my soul.
It's why I'm fighting phrase by phrase to point us to the door.
Dropping letters like a madman, leaving breadcrumbs on the floor.

This one's for all the walking dead
still holding out for more.

I saw the stream.

Clear as crystal at our feet.
Soaking every inch of earth and washing sacred on the streets.
Life is brimful to the bursting
For the weary and the thirsting
For the soul that settles still to take a drink.

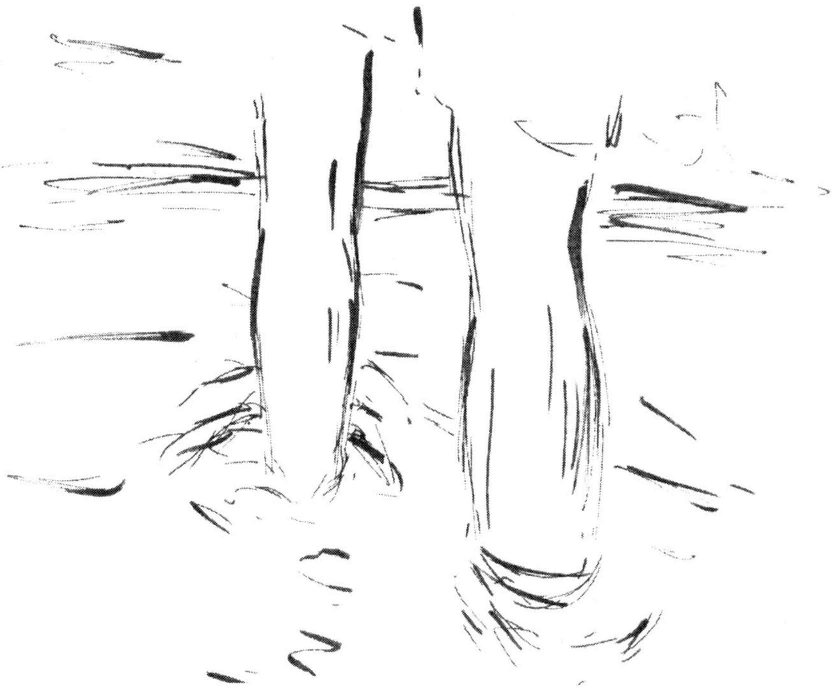

Table of contents

Acknowledgements

We don't become Human alone. This book is evidence of that. It's one thing to rattle rhymes around in your mind until they spill out as something helpful. It's another thing entirely to craft those rhymes and ramblings into the pages you're holding in your hands.

There is, I suppose, a version of this book I could have made without others. I could have held the reigns tight and pulled the curtains closed on the process to guard my artistic agenda. Thank God that I didn't.

Whatever would have come from that kind of isolation would have lacked the eye for detail and creative expertise of Jeremy Miller who crafted the design with the same kindness and patience that has marked our friendship for years. If you're a lover of fonts and appreciate visual balance, Jeremy is who you have to thank for the look and feel that pulls each word together.

Speaking of look and feel, in the early stages of writing I knew that aesthetic would be important. I wanted people to be caught up in beauty, not bogged down in analysis. For that I would need an artist. Someone who could capture the heart of my musings and sketch them to life. Tenille Douglas was the first person I thought of for the job and she did not disappoint. I pray that her illustrations would stir as much wonder in you as they have in me.

As for the writing itself, a small army of readers generously gave of their time and talent to help me edit each draft of this project into its final form. If the result has any coherence at all or spares you the verbosity of my unrestrained exuberance it is them you have to thank. To mention each person by name would need a small book of its own, but if you were part of that army you know who you are. Thank you.

Finally, there were two communities in which the seed of this idea found good ground to grow.

The first was ONE, a community of artists who set a table in the German woods where people like me could rest in God and create together. Those simple meals and sacred conversations were healing and catalytic in ways that I have yet to fully appreciate.

The second was YWAM Durban. This simple tribe on a hillside in South Africa has been my home for the past four years. They have walked with me in weakness, danced with me in strength, and graciously endured my hundredth reading of the same passage without telling me that changing a single word would probably not, in fact, change the world.

All that to say, I am grateful.

Small and simple as Human may be, I'm proud of it. It's a spark amidst the shadows, and none of it would have been possible without the many hands and hearts that have shaped it along the way.

While I pray that it would be a gift to others, I know that it has been a gift to me. I met my maker in the making. We laughed and wept together in unexpected ways as I tapped on creaky keys in the early hours of the morning. That sweet space of communion was all the reason I needed for writing.

As for you, the reader, thank you. There are many things you could have done with your time. That you chose to invest in this book is humbling.

Of course, its journey is a lot like yours. There is light in you that cannot be summoned by your strength alone. A fullness that must pass through the hearts and hands of others to find its true form. If, like me, you find that prospect daunting, may these words gift you with the grace of surrender.

Matthew Lewis

Foreword

From the moment I met Matthew over a decade ago, he struck me as someone possessing fierce longings. Since that first conversation, it has been my sacred privilege to witness him giving careful attention to these cries of his soul. Now in Human, he invites you and me to pause and attend to our below-the-surface yearnings, something he knows does not come easily for us humans to do.

In this, his first, book Matthew explores with startling freshness and provocative metaphors the inner landscape of our deepest longings. These range from our yearnings for wonder and joy to those that ache for the eternal transcendentals of truth, beauty, and goodness. Usually, quietly hidden and sometimes even tragically ignored beneath the superficialities of our hassled and hurried lives, they wait patiently to be discovered and embraced.

Matthew knows from his own searching and seeking history that when we take the time to stop and notice these longings, they breathe life into the frightening deadness of our spirit. We come alive to the light and dark in ourselves, the miracle and mystery of the person next to us, the beauty and brutality of our broken world, and most especially, to the never-ending loving tune of that old, old story that plays in the depths of our being, even when we choose not to listen.

As we follow the echoes of our truest longings into the heart of this ancient drama, we encounter Him afresh, He who was and is the Truly Human and Fully Alive One. Like His earliest followers, we are invited to trust Him with our whole selves, and in our risky trusting to discover in our own experience just who He truly is. We learn that He knows that for which most of our hearts deeply long and can alone shine the light we most desperately need for our next step along the Way.

This good news gives birth to a living hope. You and I have been desired into existence by a Great Love. We have been given one unrepeatable life. There can be fewer great tragedies than living a life characterised by meaninglessness and emptiness. Our longings remind us, however, that it doesn't have to be this way. Another kind of life is freely available to you and to me, one in which we can become more truly human and more fully alive.

Almost forty years ago, a wise Anglican nun, a veteran of the Spirit, said to me in a moment of my personal restlessness and heart-searching, "Trevor, pay close attention to your deepest longings. Do not leave them unattended. They are your bus ticket home." In this critical task, Matthew helps us to do just this!

Trevor Hudson
Minister of the Methodist Church in Southern Africa and author of SEEKING GOD: Finding Another Kind of Life with St Ignatius and Dallas Willard.

Introduction: What is this?

Not your average kind of book

None of us signed the consent form. The one so conspicuous in its absence at our moment of arrival when violent contractions pushed us, quite literally, kicking and screaming out into the world.

We didn't cast a vote or raise a hand in favour of our being. We were plunged into it without so much as a life raft and expected to swim. We didn't swim. We sank like stones into our fragility. Helpless from the start and entirely dependent on the care of others for survival.

Self-made is an illusion.

We wouldn't have lasted longer than our first few breaths without the help of others. Sadly, we forget that in our ageing.

If you're reading this, it's fair to assume that you're more than a couple of years older than the waif of a thing that gurgled for milk while wrapped tight in a blanket. By now you've probably learned a few tricks in the trade of keeping a pulse. Which is the minimum requirement for what we've come to call living.

Look beyond that however, beyond the work of mere survival to questions of meaning, purpose, and how we got here in the first place, and you quickly crash into confusion.

While we're not bad at keeping a pulse, we seem lost in understanding why we have one.

That's why I wrote this book. It's for those of us who've spent more than one morning hunched over a cup of hot coffee searching for reasons to face the day. For us pain-weary warriors still scratching for faith in the dirt and scanning waves that shake the earth while mumbling softly beneath our breath: "A little help here, please?"

For those sick of the survival slums that frame our days who hope beyond hope for the faint promise of real living.

This is a book about being Human.

Except it's not your average kind of book. It doesn't resolve as books are prone to do. Yes, you'll find an unfolding story with each turning of the page, and some beautiful thoughts that offer themselves up like a cool breeze in a world of fluster. But in general, this is more a wild jungle of a book than it is a curated garden.

Humanity isn't easily tamed.

It's better flung wide across a broad canvas of description than crammed tight into the cramped space of the defined.

So, if you're settled in surface-level-living-scrolling-sound-bites-on-socials, this might not be your preference.

But if you ache to dance in the tension of transcendence and probe the depths of a wide-open soul, then maybe...just maybe...you'll find healing in the pages of this book that I never meant to write.

A happy accident for which I must blame Germany.

Some curious force

I was there in 2023 with a podcast in my ears and feet that walked their way through a forest. The air was crisp that morning in the little town of Herrnhut; it's one of my favourite places on the planet. The walls between this world and the other seem thinner there somehow[1]. Those slender streets, where bakery windows light up the early hours like a warm lantern and soften the winter with the smell of fresh bread, seem spacious to me. There's enough room in the air to drop the gathered baggage of your being and step out into something more substantial.

I took a deep breath beside a stream as I walked. It carved its way through trees that towered tall into a canopy cathedral where birds chirped hymns to greet the dawning. That's when the podcast in my ears dropped a seed into the soil of me. It was an orderly thought.

But, like all seeds worth planting, it had a forest of its own packed tight into a tiny shell.

Before long, it started sprouting shoots. Slowly at first, a poem here, a story there. Then far more quickly. Thought after beautiful thought began bursting like blossoms on branches that sprawled in every direction. Order gave way to an explosion as phrases lit up my mind like literary fireworks. It was a creative riot that, if I'm honest, probably had more to do with the soil than the seed. By that I mean, I've never been one for monotone musing or straight-line thinking. There's a carnival in me that I've often tried to keep on a leash for the sake of being productive. Not this time. This time I didn't try to walk the proverbial dog.

This time I let the dog walk me.

I nearly lost my arm in the process. It was pulled clean out of the socket more than once by some curious force that yanked my attention in every unexpected direction –

A 'Ferris wheel on acid'.

I remember almost tripping over those words as they fell through my fingers onto the keyboard. I leaned back and let out the kind of laugh that rumbles up from the deepest parts of the belly. Good glory, I can still feel it now! What on earth is a 'Ferris wheel on acid', and how on earth (or heaven) did it find its way into my mind? On reflection, I think it's fair to say that I was, at best, a partner in the discovery of these words.

In a way that I hope is not too mystical to mention straight out the gate, I really did feel led through what has been the most wonderful adventure. It was as if another mind, heart, or hand was guiding me down pathways I never would have found on my own. Some of them turned out to be dead ends that I had to backspace my way out of. But even those were not wasted explorations. They stored up treasure in me that might never make it past the secret place of my soul.

Then, there were those paths that wound their way through clumsy words and cliché phrases to settle into something that felt like an oasis. Like sweet streams in a searching world reminding me of my humanity with each sip of the sentences that filled them. It's all been a gift that I couldn't keep to myself.

I think we all need some reminding of what it means to be human.

To the journey

And so, I offer this forest to you. My hope is that you would experience it as I have – with surrendered curiosity that leads to adventure, and the willingness to drink deeply of the source that inspired it all in the first place.

You might start at the beginning and walk, step by step, to the end. It's a tapestry in that way. Each thread of thought weaves into the next to make an image of the reason that we're here.

The reason that we're anywhere at all.

Or you might find yourself pulled into poems and stories in ways that seem random at first. Feel free to colour outside the lines in these moments. Those subtle invitations are probably not random at all and might call for lingering beyond what you're used to. Lingering, by the way, is the appropriate response to many of the worlds that these words are building.

I imagine phrases worn down and faded from the frequent visitations of those who receive them as gifts.

All along the way, you'll find excercises to help you pause and reflect. From one pilgrim to another, don't rush past these. A mountain is more than its summit[2], and even the deepest of truths are only so helpful when they skim across the surface of our lives. Clarity comes in the settling. So, move slowly as you follow each excercise into the deeper contours of your story.

Finally, wherever this journey takes you and however you walk the path, I pray that you would find seeds of your own wrapped up in each sentence and that some of them would grow into tall trees and canopies made up of all that it means to be Human.[3]

In a world that seems to have lost so much of itself to the noise of sick stories, we could use all the Humans we can get.

One: Connection

Honest

They say we don't rise higher than the stories we believe in. I don't know who *they* are exactly, or why we trust these opinionated strangers so blindly, but I think I agree with them on the stories. Stories have shaped me since birth. I couldn't tell you what they were (they blur around the edges in the rear-view mirror of my memory), but I can tell you how they made me feel. How they made me shrink small or stand tall in the unfolding seasons of life.

Some stories grew fear in the hard-to-reach places of my internal world. I've been afraid for a long time. Not the kind of fear that sends you hiding under blankets while thunder shakes the windows. More the kind that flings your mouth wide open in silence to build walls with words that cover up your aching insecurity. I wish I could say all that was behind me. It isn't, not completely. I've slain a dragon or two with truths that I've picked up along the way, but some monsters don't die easily.

In so many ways I'm still a little boy, afraid of being known but not loved.

That's why this is daunting. Writing a book, I mean. I've needed more than one deep breath to wade through the fear of other people's opinions. Rejection is a word that stalks me, which might seem melodramatic for some letters on a page – it probably is. But that's me. I swim through this world in an ocean of emotion that needs the navigation skills of a seaworthy captain.

So, since we're already neck-deep in oversharing, I'm insecure about my age. I'm not old per se, but I'm not young, and I'm hoping that this book is not some vain mid-life attempt to outrun my impending ordinariness. Because I'm afraid of being ordinary, almost as much as I'm afraid of being spectacular, almost as much as I'm afraid of dying, which – ironically – makes me a little afraid of living.

Some have told me to be careful. They're concerned that all this talk of fear might manifest its own paralysis. I hear that. And yet, I think there's a difference between manifestation and acknowledgement.

Faith and denial are not synonymous terms, and our shadows do the most damage when buried in the grave of suppression (more on that later).

I started balding in my mid-twenties and raised the white flag to the razor around the age of thirty. Now I'm gathering wrinkles like collectibles. I know because I see them each morning in the mirror which, depending on the day, can unleash a tiny existential crisis. Think Oppenheimer for the ego.

I still exercise. One small step for man. But not before I stretch. I stretch a lot. I stretch like a contortionist trying to fit into a shoe box just so I can break a sweat without injury. Last year I went for a check-up at the optometrist who calmly told me I needed glasses. Luckily, some teenager scrolling through TikTok assured me that glasses were on trend.
So, there's that.

I'm not sharing all this for sympathy – far from it. What I'm hoping for is honesty.

Not only mine, but yours. Honesty is as vital as oxygen. It excavates the true self from pretence and builds a bridge to the connection we so desperately need.[4] To quote that smiling saint, Desmond Tutu:
"We can only be human together."[5]

Which is, of course, the challenge. Honesty (the means of our much-needed connection) is a rare commodity these days. It's harder to find than a fistful of diamonds in the dirt. None of us look like the glam filter on our Instagram reel and I don't know about you, but my mornings don't start with a soundtrack.

When people ask me how I am, I usually say that I'm fine. But honestly, I can't remember the last time I was just 'fine'. I'm generally some combination of things that I only half understand after processing them out loud. But who has time for that – processing, I mean? There's no room for such indulgence in an ocean of busyness. It's why we settle for two-dimensional platitudes over transactional handshakes designed to grease the wheels of getting things done.

That's part of the problem.

We're addicted to getting things done, or at least to the appearance of getting things done. Our roots run deep in the soil of a story designed to blur the boundaries between the production line and the contours of our souls. If you still believe in such a thing... a soul that is. Which you might not, and that is another part of the problem. According to ***them***, we don't rise higher than the stories we believe in.

And soulless stories place very low ceilings on our lives.

Say it scared

All of this is killing us. We see it in the escalating body count that floods our feed with each headline, and in the subtle, sparkless gaze marring the faces of entire generations who are strung thin on a digital drug deal gone bad.

I thought about this on the train the other day. It was delayed by an hour due to debris on the track. An hour. Due to debris. I wondered if we could make that train driver president of the world or something. Maybe he could help us find a handbrake for our lives before we drive ourselves off an existential cliff.

This brings me to the point of these words. I'm not here to curse the darkness. I'm sure we're all aware of what's broken and complaining doesn't water dry ground to grow hope. I'm here to light a candle, shift the needle, or somehow dig loose the avalanche that has settled so heavily over our collective consciousness.

You see, I think we're about a stone's throw away from species-wide amnesia and this is my small attempt to remind us of what it means to be Human.

I know these are big dreams for a man still afraid of being seen. But the thing is, I found new wrinkles in the mirror this morning and next year I will officially be too old to wear skinny jeans. It's science. So even if it's just for me and a handful of others, and even though I don't know if guys like me should be doing things like this, I've decided to do it anyway.

Fear, it turns out, is part of what it means to be Human.

It's right up there with joy and grief, hope and despair, doubt, belief, and courage – which, I'm told, is not the absence of fear but the defiance of it. So, here I am, ready to say it scared because I heard that small words with small faith can move big mountains into the great sea and I have some mountains that need moving.[6]

What about you?

Before we strike a match and light this flame, "How are you, honestly?"

Pause

Silence

Find a quiet place. I know that this can be challenging, but trust me, it's worth the effort. Once you find your place (This might be anywhere from a bathroom cubicle to a park bench, to that saving grace of noise-cancelling headphones on the subway) settle into the silence and begin to breathe deeply. In through the nose, out through the mouth. Three seconds in, three seconds out is usually a good rhythm. Do this for at least a minute.

- As you start to relax, give yourself permission to feel. I know this might seem like a strange thing to say, but when last did you unclench the tight fist in your gut and simply allow your feelings to flow?

- Pay attention to the emotions that stir up in you. They may come quickly or slowly. They may be welcome emotions or ones you would rather avoid. Don't try to control them or analyse them, simply make room for them.

- When you're ready, choose one of these emotions and name it with a word. I am feeling… (any word but 'fine' will do).

- Finally, get curious about that emotion. What might it be trying to tell you about how you are in this moment?

Two: The Question

Allergic

Silence can feel awkward, like the dis-ease of sharing a park bench with someone you don't know, or the urge to avoid eye contact by being overly interested in the ceiling of a cramped elevator. Silence barely makes it through the door these days before it sends us running to the digital appendage of our smartphone where we mainline distraction as a sedative. I wonder why. Is it because, just like that person on the park bench, silence is the stranger of our age? Are we simply hooked on adrenaline, or is there something deeper we're avoiding? I wonder what waits beyond the settling dust that makes us tremble so.

Whatever it is, this allergy is a tragedy for us all.

Wonder

It reminds me of a lake in Japan. I sat there on a jetty one evening as steam from the coffee in my hand swayed slowly into the crisp twilight air. The sun dropped low behind the horizon and spilt out a final gift before fading. A kind of encore for those with eyes to see, glowing amber and soft pink washed over a dusty blue sky and skipped across the gently lapping water.

A family stood waiting on the charcoal pebble beach, a mother, a father, and two little girls with hair as dark as the encroaching night and matching pink dresses sewn from the same pallet that lit the lapping waters. I could feel their joy as they dug deep in tiny pockets to pull out handfuls of duck pellets. They hurled them into the lake fist by miniature fist. Each handful landed like buckshot on the glass kaleidoscope of colour that had become the water. Ripples ran in every direction, colliding in a liquid mosh pit while swans swam in to join the party.

Grateful quacks echoed into the air mixing with the glee-filled laughter of little girls still showering swans with pellets. Something resonated in me as I looked on from my bobbing jetty. It was as if a harmony, humming in the same key as my own deepest longings, woke laughter in my soul and pulled it to the surface of my being. I was giggling over my steaming coffee, like a child – like those children, the ones who shone brighter in their grateful innocence than a sunset ever could.

I remember thinking how alive and light and... Human it all felt.

Those girls, so free from themselves and lost in the gift of the moment, changed duck pellets and squawking swans into something that felt like a miracle. The tragedy is that most people on the beach that day missed it. Instead of drinking in the deep wonder all around them, they were lost in selfie sticks at golden hour trying to capture the perfect post. I think we're in danger of the same thing.

I think we're prone to miss the wonder.

Which brings us back to silence.

Strong drink

There is life beyond the numbness of distraction, a fullness that we crave in the depths of our being. Silence helps us find it. Like a pathway of descent that cracks wide the floor of the world, silence helps us settle into substance. You might not call it silence. It's a gift that goes by many names. Stillness, slowness, or attention might be some that are more familiar to you.

I imagine them as three old sages sitting by a stream somewhere.

The sound of trickling water fills the air like a deep breath. Words feel weighty and sacred. It's not the kind of place where you run your mouth to push back the quiet.

They greet me with a simple smile as I drop down slowly beside them. Stillness shuffles gently through a patched-up pocket and pulls out a fist full of pebbles. Slowness nods a single nod with welcome in her eyes. All the while, Attention stares – with focused expectation – at the flowing stream, the floating leaves, and the shifting shadows rolling free with every gentle gust of wind.

Like a person looking skyward on a busy street,
his unbroken gaze makes me wonder what I'm missing.

I pick a few pebbles from the patient hand of Stillness. Without a thought, I throw one. It skips twice across the water. I throw again. Four skips this time. A third pebble. Then a fourth. Each one has a few more skips than the last. Stillness has no shortage of pebbles in his patched-up pocket it seems. Skip by skip, ripple by ripple, each throw helps me drink deep of the wonder gathering in pools at my feet. I look left at my three new friends. They are smiling more broadly now. Even Attention breaks his gaze to share a glance of grateful recognition.

It's strong drink, this wonder is.

Those once shallow pools are now a swirling sea, washing wonder over everything. Potent as a potion and humble as a saint, it subtly sneaks into each breath and floods my lungs with gratitude. Gratitude, persuasive and persistent as it is, starts slowly stirring me sober. Or making me drunk. Either way, it pries wide my sleeping eyes to see the gift of where I am, the gift of where I've always been. Here... now... in this very moment.

I am firmly planted in the ordinary magic
of the earth beneath my feet.

Thank God, I didn't miss it. Thank God for three new friends and a pocket full of pebbles.

The standoff

Let me say it one more time for those at the back.

Our lives are brimful to bursting with wonder.

But true as that is, sometimes saying it out loud still feels like a handbrake of words in my mouth. There are days when the idea of wonder barely gets off the floor before it's tripped up by a strong dose of reality. Perhaps you can relate. Perhaps, like me, you've felt the wet blanket of a broken world dampen hope and hamstring the spring in your step before you take your first breath of the morning. You're not alone in your dejection. None of us are.

The limping ghosts of our dull-eyed ancestors serve as tragic reminders of just how fragile wonder can be.

I can almost sense the smug condescension of tyrants and despots through the ages staring me down from the blood-drenched halls of history. I imagine them smirking and snickering behind calloused hands at the naivety of believing that anything stronger than cynicism might fight its way to the surface of us. I hear their 'measured call to reason'. They, and those who punt their poison propaganda, lie through bleached white teeth while sipping a cognac.

"This is all there is..." they say.

"These soot-covered dreams and stunted souls are just the way things are, the way they've always been. Hate is the heartbeat around here and hoping for hope is... a child's game."

Then squaring up to me and pointing a chubby finger straight in my face, they try to intimidate the wonder right out of my stiffening spine. "You sir, have no business striking sparks where you can't start a fire."

It's a persuasive speech, perfectly delivered to stamp hope right out of disruptive insurgents like me. For a moment I'm tempted to believe it. I feel myself shrinking into their chokehold of intimidation until something snaps me out of it – a whisper. Strong as thunder, light as a breeze, it shakes me free of fear in a moment.

"It's worth it.
Wonder is worth the flames that it is forged in".

Courage rises warm and fast as I brush off the lies that have gathered like cobwebs. I'm standing taller now, holding fistfuls of flint and ready for the fire even as cries of "Peter Pan!" ring out around me. Let them scream. I won't be struck down by those who frame faith as delusion.

I choose a braver way.

Child-like as it may seem to the powers that be, I choose to believe that cynics aren't peddling wisdom, that hope is not naïve, and that sometimes – just sometimes – the child-like are the ones who see things most clearly.[7]

All that to say, I'm here to find the wonder and
I'm hoping you will join me.

Pushing back a hurricane

Let's start with you. You're a dirt-breathed heartbeat still standing in the stir of existence. That is no easy task. To stay standing I mean. I saw a palm tree bent over in a hurricane, tenaciously gripping the earth with every ounce of its might. I thought, *Why don't we have more monuments to palm trees? Maybe they could stir some courage for those of us holding on in the hurricanes that we all shudder through sooner or later in the sheer act of survival.*

Yes, all of us.

I've poured out my soul with more than one stranger over tea, coffee, or freshly pressed sugarcane on crushed ice in Cambodia. We've wondered, these strangers and I, at the peculiarity of it all. Our faces worn like stone in the wind, we have laughed and cried in deep recognition of our common journey.

I thank God for them – companions on the way who, most often, have been through more than I could imagine and are far braver than I believed possible. I'm sure it wouldn't take more than a cup of pressed sugarcane to find out that you're a lot like them in that way – brave, I mean.

Your story might not look like mine or that of the young man reaching for tinned soup on the top shelf at your local grocery store. But I think you understand the hurricane. So, breathe deeply, just for a moment, and savour the sweet mercy that has you still standing... or sitting... or stumbling slowly forward.

You, my friend, are a palm tree pushing back a hurricane, and don't you forget it!

Grounded

I'm sure, like me, you've gathered the scars and wrinkles that roll in with time. Those storm clouds that build on a summer afternoon, heavy with the dark promise of a downpour. You're probably crammed full of stories. Most people are when we're wise enough to listen. Stories of scraped knees, hot tea, simple sandwiches on picnic grass, and dishes – some that sparkle clean, freshly packed on the kitchen shelf, and others that rise high in the sink like Everest casting their humbling shadow over your best attempts to have it all together. Don't dismiss any of it in your pining after grandeur. The scars, the stories, the dishes. All of it is a gift.

These monuments to the mundane are essential to the work of staying grounded, something which any of us hoping to be Human must ultimately be.

Staying grounded saves us from floating off into the clouds on our inflated egos, or scrambling for the bomb shelters of pretence when insecurities start whistling overhead. It holds us cheek to cheek with the dark, familiar dirt of the earth where ants scramble skittishly over our searching fingers scrolling patterns in the topsoil. There, low and humble with the world that we call home, is where we glimpse the gold that can't be seen at thirty thousand feet. The good stuff.

Like laughter.

Laugh

I hope that you have laughed.
The kind that melts you down to a puddle.
Grabbing your gut
Wiping your eyes
And clenching your bladder tight as a vice
So not to wet your pants.

I hope you've laughed valleys deep into your skin,
Carved cavern creases for the light to flow within
And trace shadows thick as frames
Across your artwork smile.

I hope you've laughed like an earthquake.
With deep, joyful, convulsions that shake loose gathering dust
And send gold flecks dancing free in the morning glow.
I hope that you have laughed enough to know

This life is worth your living.

And don't forget the tears. Don't buy the lie that shrinks you down to the one-dimensional half-life of a comfort seeker. No, you were made for living, and that's a juice that's worth the squeeze. But sometimes, the juice is in the squeezing.

So...

Tears

I hope that you have cried.
Not just droplets,
Those that fall gentle over the heart's brim in shimmering beads.
But the deluge.

I hope you've cried to breaking point,
Crumpled foetal on the ground,
Gasping desperate as weak strength caved in
To the flood that flows from deep laceration.

I hope you've cried a river,
Cried an ocean,
Cried the earth itself away
Until you were sprawled empty on the bathroom floor.

I hope you've cried,
Not for your pain,
Pain is gravity
And needs no incitement in coming.

No, I hope you've cried yourself sane,
With great bucket-loads of healing.

There is, I've found, a strange beauty buried in the places we call ash.
And tears dig deep through messy lives
To lure it to the surface.

So, I hope that you have cried.

All that to say (and I hope you're starting to see) that right here in the strange mix of luminous affliction we call living, is all the wonder we could ask for. It's packed tight into the simplest of things waiting for wise eyes to pay attention. Which is something we're unlikely to do if we're more interested in loading our time like a pack-mule than savouring it like a fine wine.

Wonder eludes the frantic.

So, perhaps, instead of striving to get ahead, or move up, or however you might frame that ancient temptation to power and prestige over purpose and meaning, we might pause to ask some deeper questions of ourselves. Questions like: "Where are we from?", "Why are we here?", and "Where is all of this going?" or to put it more succinctly, perhaps we might slow down to consider:

"What does it mean to be Human?"

Pause

Get curious

Before you rush on to the next chapter, take a moment to linger here. As you did before, slowly settle into the silence in a quiet, comfortable space.

When you are ready scan back over what you have just read about wonder and the question that finds us when we make room for it to rise *(What does it mean to be human?)*

- Let your eyes drift over the words and as they do, take note of which words or phrases stand out to you. It might be helpful to write one or two of them down.

- When you're done, look at the words you have written down and choose one of them. Why do you think this caught your attention?
  (There's often an invitation hiding in the things we notice.
  Not everyone stopped for that sunrise, paused in that silence,
  or picked up the phrase in that poem. You did. Why?)

- When you are ready, write about what you're thinking as you consider this word or phrase. What might it have to teach you about yourself?

Three: Learning to dance

Cottonmouth

It's risky business, making room to consider what it means to be Human. With enough space to breathe, it's a question that could burn the whole world to the ground; or maybe just all the world's too thin to face the furnace. That hasn't stopped us from trying for an answer though. Pry open a dictionary and you'll find the word 'human' defined as (drum roll please): "Relating to or characteristic of a human being".[8]

I got cottonmouth reading that sentence.

How did we fall from the cosmic carnival of us into the doldrums of a definition as bland as a cardboard sandwich? It's like a painted portrait on limp paper in faded grey. No flame to fill the eyes. No blush to frame the face. Not wrong, but not nearly enough to be true. Which is to be expected, I guess. It's no easy task trying to sum up our fullness – think about it...

Bottle the ocean

We sit silent in wide-eyed wonder
While constellations trace their way across the pitch-black sky.
We breathe deep the scent symphony of springtime blossom.
We huddle warm by flickering flame,
As crisp winter mornings wake the wild and bird songs fill the air.

We love and make love.

We wipe wet eyes as babies cry, mothers sigh, and loved ones die.
We eat,
Ice cream,
Lick-by-mouth-watering-lick as pecan praline and salted caramel drip sticky down a wafer cone.

And, even though we try,
We have yet to plumb the depths of our own infinite selves.
So we reach for the heavens and pull down fistfuls of stardust because:

How do you bottle the ocean?

Radiant shadows

Who can blame the dictionary for playing it safe? Like children rummaging hand over fist through an oversized toy box, the magnitude of this question is enough to stump the finest philosophers among us.

What does it mean to be Human indeed?

At our best, we stand with full chests under the banner of being humanitarians. At our worst, we mumble softly – with shifting eyes – that universal pardon of, “I’m only human.” We heal our world to wholeness with one hand while stripping it bare with the other. We are victor and villain, radiant shadows scrambling for solid ground in our quest for self-definition. And that is a part of our problem.

Self-definition.

The pianist

I was in a subway in Europe. It was busy. People were crammed in tighter than luggage on the back seat of an SUV. It gets hot in such small spaces. Especially when you're pressed closer to some stranger than you've ever been to your own mother. When it gets hot, people get cranky. There's only so much bumping, squeezing, and accidental heel stamping you can take before, even if it doesn't burst out of your mouth, irritation hangs on your face like a lopsided painting.

I wish I could tell you that the quiet gave me some relief that day. It didn't. It was loud down there. Even through the final defence of my noise-cancelling headphones, I could hear the cacophony bouncing off faded tiles like a Ferris wheel on acid.

High-pitched laughter shattered the space over my left shoulder. Some kid screaming blue murder in search of a Fizz Pop melted the air to my right. A sinus clearer here, a Coke can cracker there, and the wheezy breathing just behind me of some dude who had long forgotten the concept of social distancing. Then, just when I thought that this madness had brought its A-game to the mayhem, the clanking and clunking of a piano rang out from somewhere off in the distance.

Drifting eerily over the sound carnage erupting all around me, it landed straight in my lap and made me literally beg, in silent pleas of agony, for the train to arrive. The train did not arrive. And every 30 seconds or so, that clanking-clunking piano would jab me in the ribs with an off note that some sugar-high child was no doubt smashing out on its flinching ivory keys.

Then suddenly, silence settled like a cool mist – at least from the piano. A minute or two went by in what was now, comparatively, a manageable level of sound carnage. Until I heard it again – the piano that is. Except this time it was different. I imagine that a pair of haggard parents had found their manic children and restrained them, because this time the notes drifting over the mayhem didn't feel like a gut punch from a boxer.

They felt like... freedom.

In place of the dull clanking-clunking torture, came a melody. It was beautiful. It flowed like fresh running water over drooping shoulders and shuffling feet. I felt my lopsided face painting pull level with every rise and fall of its tumbling tones. I was not alone.

I noticed Coke can guy pause mid-sip to lift his dark eyes over wide-brim glasses toward the soothing sound. Fizz Pop kid slowly stopped writhing and just lay there, wide-eyed and still on the filthy subway floor. Sinus lady was on her tiptoes. She was trying to grab a glimpse over the high-pitched laughers who stared with her now in the direction of whatever was filling the air with such welcome relief. As for the wheezer, I don't know if he knew it, but he was nearly holding his breath while a small smile cracked his stubbly face like a sunbeam.

For the briefest of moments, I forgot where I was; I think we all did. Closing my eyes and tucking both thumbs tight under my backpack straps, I swayed gently to the enfolding melody.

It felt like a long hug from an old friend that you haven't seen in ages.

Suddenly, screeching brakes from the approaching train ripped a hole in the calm and threw me back into the subway. Without skipping a beat, the Ferris wheel gears began to grind again while I stepped off the platform and onto the waiting carriage. I was surprisingly grateful. That melody found me in the mayhem and led me to a hidden gift. As the train slowly pulled away and new victims shuffled into the empty spaces we had left behind, a simple thought settled down beside me:

I guess you can play the piano however you want to, but only some ways feel like music.

Handmade

We're a bit more complicated than a Steinway, don't you think? Consider the brain. It is an intricate web of 86 billion neurons. Each one, a star in some cosmic orchestra dancing with thousands of others, trading electric whispers of thought and emotion. Then there's the heart. It rhythmically pounds percussive beats over 100,000 times a day. These rivers of crimson life flow in our veins and we barely stop to notice. All of this – this marvel that is us – recites a detailed script penned by DNA. Six feet (two metres) of it packed into every single one of the thirty trillion cells that build the bodies we call home (I'll let you do the math).

We are a long list of sheer impossibility trailing off on the floor before our feet, going on, and on, and on, and on. An accident? Perhaps. We might stuff ourselves into the cramped cave of that conclusion, but not without strain.

We would have to forget, you see,
that masterpieces don't make themselves.

Behind every portrait is a painter. Symphony's flow in time to the flick and fall of impassioned conductors. That Lego castle, rising high in pride of place on the dining room table, didn't build itself.

Yes, technically, it is possible that we're just the incredible consequence of cosmic collision. Time plus matter plus chance and all that. But I just don't have enough faith to believe it.

I think we're handmade.

Knit together, strand by strand, in the deep dark of the womb.[9] Our stretched-wide breathing and bright-eyed blinking all sway to the blueprint beat of someone else's drum. Which brings us back to our problem.

Self-definition.

The room next door

Yes, I guess we can play the piano however we want to. We can slam the keys of our souls until the world overflows with the clanking-clunking noise of our stubborn misdirection. Pick your headline.

But just because it's sound, doesn't mean that it's music.

No, music is what's happening in the room next door. That ancient place where the very first DJ dropped a beat so fresh that it pushed back the darkness and hasn't stopped since.

You can still hear it if you listen.

It's muffled through the wall, but you can feel it in the floor with a base tone so raw that it thumps like a heartbeat. Wait a little longer and you'll start to hear the dancing, the samba, tango, waltz and more, with just enough *Indlamu*[10] to kick up the dust of the African soil.

They're dancing next door, and we are invited to join them – step by life-giving step, one flowing flawlessly into the next; each divinely designed to keep us from crushing toes while staring at our own fumbling feet. You might say that we're neck deep in an endless celebration that's only gaining steam as we speak.

You might say that being Human means learning to dance to that beat.

Pause

Now we're dancing

If there is a 'base-beat in the room next door', an ultimate rhythm for our being, it's likely that our greatest peace, deepest joy, and moments of feeling most fully alive are those that are aligned with that rhythm. It's a helpful practice to learn to pay attention to our lives and notice the moments when we felt most aligned and those where we did not.

- Find a quiet place and take a moment to settle into silence. Breathe slowly in and out for about a minute.

- When you are ready, let the events of the last week run through your mind like a movie reel. See yourself waking up, having coffee, interacting with people, and going about your work.

- Don't try to control this, just let the 'movie reel' run. Pay attention to moments and experiences that bring back feelings of joy, peace, and a sense of deep fulfilment.

- Choose one of those moments and consider what it was about this moment that made you feel this way. You might want to write your thoughts down.

- Finally, consider how you might live more intentionally in the week to come, to make room for more moments like these. This might include things like emptying an over-busy schedule, being more present to the people who fill your day, or pausing to appreciate small gifts of simple beauty as they arrive.

Four: Truth

Footpaths for the brave

Truth is what we call it – that base beat in the room next door inviting us to dance. You might not have heard it framed like that before, without the grainy images of box-checking and rule-keeping that flatline a pulse faster than textbooks slapping a cold counter. But it is Truth, and Truth is fascinating.

More than a mould to fit into, Truth is a longing to explore.

And it is not alone. We're crammed full of longings. Things set deep as the heart, and deeper, that have been squashed silent under the low ceiling of the thin stories we live into.[11] But pull the roof off those stories with a question that calls us to substance (like, "What does it mean to be human?") and these longings start breaching the surface of us faster than beach balls breaking water, each one an invitation like signposts in a fog or footpaths for the brave that rise to lead us into lives that feel like fullness.[12]

Stockholm syndrome

Truth is one of the feistier longings within us. It isn't Switzerland; it tends to split a room by picking fights with every backyard bully still trying to hold our heads over the toilet bowl of confusion. That's why it seldom makes the guest list at our parties, its invite gets lost in the mail because, if we're honest, we would rather skip the drama of confrontation. We're tangled tight by lesser stories that hold our allegiance even as they harm us.

Stockholm syndrome is what they call it.

Falling

Lies flicker bright
As cell phones light
The shadows shrouding weary faces.

Bags hang heavy on barren eyes,
As filters try to colour-clean the aching disappointment
Now rising on a tide of epiphany.

We are not enough.

They said we would be.
That free-dumb choir still chanting its liberation anthem,
A coup against the captor they call truth.

Dripped in gleaming gold
Ripped from the ground of our slowly crumbling souls
These 'heroes' bathe in our dopamine
Slug down our serotonin
And feast frenzy on joy tapped straight from our turbulent minds.

They cry, *"Vive la Résistance!"*
And we cry with them.
Hurled by pride from the firm ground of sanity.

We're alive in the free fall... until we're not,
Until we're stunned sober by the imminent earth beneath
And blind eyes finally see.

There is no freedom here,
Only falling.
And gravity is no slave to our preference.

A better story

Gravity: the inescapable proof that not all things are up for negotiation. Hard data for the lingering sceptic confirming that Truth, like concrete, is what we crash into when we're wrong.

Wrong is not a word we hear very often.

It's why we're stumbling around on the fractured ground of self-definition. We've written feeble stories for ourselves that simply aren't working in any way that matters. From our hearts that are aching to the world that we're breaking, all of it is shaking us awake asking us to pay attention.

We are wrong in so many ways.

We're plummeting in free fall as concrete rushes toward us. We desperately need, and ache, and long for a better story. Not just one that soothes the senses, stuffing down sedatives to fight the harsh light of what's real. We need a story that's True.[13] The kind that moves to the groove of the beat in the room next door. Thankfully, such a story exists.[14]

Imagine with me.

The Old Story

We lean low like children.
Huddled tight with straining eyes to spy
Through a keyhole.

Our hushed whispers echo soft in the cavernous void beyond,
Where time itself stands ready,
Pregnant and poised like a tight, coiled, spring,
Waiting... for the unravelling.

Spirit hovers thick over churning sea.
Deep dark hangs ominous but ready to bow the knee.
To a word.

Light!
Let there be light.

This spoken detonation
Scatters shards free across the rising earth.

Waters subsiding
Night and day dividing
Heavens aligning
As Truth is designing life.

Leaves, limbs
Feathers, fins
And beasts
That tread fresh tracks on virgin dirt.

The dirt.

Where time, still infant and zealous, must pause.
Where hands form
And Truth bends low,
To breathe the dust human.

The memory

Can you feel that? Those joy sparks in your stomach cracking a smile across your face without asking for permission. There seems to be a whispered affirmation within us that bears witness to this story through the keyhole. Beyond the cold intellectualism of slick sentences or strong objection, there is – if we're brave enough to be honest – a kind of visceral familiarity that stretches wide its morning arms in the wake of these words.

For me at least, and many I've spoken to, hearing the story of dirt-breathed-human feels like looking through a dusty photo album. We turn page by faded page as faces and places remind us of the worlds we've left behind, of where we came from.

Similarly, our heart vaults are full of faded recollections. They're buried beneath the clutter of busy and distracted lives. They're washed over by broken intentions and wayward desires. But they are there, ready for words like these to rouse them. When we slow down to listen, this story speaks its light until it doesn't feel like a story anymore.

It feels like a memory.

And what do we remember? Not high in the attic of the mind, but deeper. What do we remember in the place that our age has so violently tried to deny, called the Spirit, in that basement deep part of us that still holds the transcendent treasure of eternal things?

I think we remember the forming... the breath... the strong hands and whispered words that spoke new life into our dust bowl bodies at first as they uttered one simple phrase:

"In our image."[15]

I think we remember the Truth of what it means to be Human. At least part of it. That we are not the maker but the made. We are hand-crafted for more than vain glory and fading praise. We are shaped like mirrors, born to display nothing less than the ultimate reality that some still call God. This is why we can't settle. It's why nothing in this world satisfies our soul-deep longing. We are not made for this world but for the maker of worlds,[16] and "TikTok star" is a far fall from the heights of such glory.

We can try to bed down on inferior ground and skulk around like shadows. We can turn our gaze from the persistent light in fear of what we might find there... or what might find us. We can shake our heads and try to forget but, in the end, the hope of home won't stay buried long in the shallow graves that distraction can dig.

There are always people rising from the dead.

There, amidst the mud and the mess, are those who fan their longings into flame with deep breaths of surrender. They choose a kind of dying that leads them into living[17] until they step like salt on earth and pull everlasting flavours from fading concrete floors.[18]

The brave ones

The brave ones.
Those flickering flames in history's grey who've let their longings breathe.
Bent low on yielded knees,
Their hands washed clean of mud pies.

They charge the beckoning seas
Like children,
And chains fall free as they do.

Their bodies bleed crimson.
Flung heavy by turbulent tides
While inside they rise.

Tall as trees
With roots pressed deep.

In the garden.

There, with the first of us,
They stand safe beneath Love's gaze
And ancient words speak fresh affirmation.

"Good. Yes, this is very good.

Pause

Shallow graves

Similarly to how our deepest joy, peace and fulfilment are found in moments of alignment with Truth, so too our deepest pain, anxiety and disappointment can be found in moments of misalignment with Truth. Moments when we are living in alignment with lies.

- As with the exercises before, settle into silence by breathing deeply in and out for about a minute.
- When you are ready, allow the past week to run through your mind like a movie reel.
- This time, instead of paying attention to those things that brought you joy and peace, pay attention to those things that caused you pain, anxiety, fear or disappointment.
- Choose one of these moments and ask yourself what it was about this moment that made you feel this way. You might want to write this down.
- Now go a little deeper. Is there perhaps a lie that you are believing about yourself, others, or this situation that has made you feel this way? You might want to write this down.
- Finally, if there is a lie that you have recognised, what Truth could you choose to live into instead of this lie in the week ahead when similar moments arise?

Five: Goodness

Good enough to be Human

Sometimes goodness is the last word we would use to describe ourselves or others, and yet it is precisely what we most deeply long to be. A fact that's easily forgotten in the hum-drum rhythm of ordinary days. That's why we need to stop and ask our question of what it means to be Human.

We need to wonder long enough at the meaning of our being to notice the rumbling.

Yes, the rumbling. That soul-deep-stirring we sense as our longing for Goodness rises like a giant from within. It snaps leads and shakes free debris in its waking, to point us to that footpath in the fog and beckon us to walk it.

It's a sight that stirs defiance. When we see it, we're moved to snap leads of our own, to break ties with the lies that bind us to prestige, power, and greed.

The greater the height of its rising, the longer the shadow it throws over our need for flawless skin pulled tighter than satin sheets and six-pack abs as rock hard as the gold streets that should rise high into our ever-growing mountains of money.

Goodness shames that story, the one I hope you're starting to see dripping poison into your tea each morning. The trend, which keeps rewarding virtue signals with likes while loudly applauding the appearance of character without any desire for the substance thereof.

Goodness closes the curtain on cheap theatrics to call forth a much older story.

That one we spied through a keyhole. The story of dirt-breathed human where Love sees the fresh form it has fashioned and calls it Good from the start.

Before our mirror souls were covered thick with deceptive dust and rebellious amnesia. Before shame banished us to wild places where we laboured on the land by the sweat of our brow. Before greed bent us crooked and, like an arrow flung free without aim, we missed the mark entirely.[19] Before that great falling, our unveiled faces burned bright with an image, and it was Good. Not just Good, but very Good.[20] The kind of Good that painted a waiting world brilliant with colour and calmed the cosmos, which sighed in relief at our arrival.

In *The Old Story*, the first of us was Good enough to be Human.

What does that mean? What is this Goodness calling from the core of our being? There are no easy answers to that question I'm afraid. Much like Truth, and most transcendent things, Goodness is not ours to define (that's where we went wrong in the first place). It won't shrink small for our convenience or allow itself to be broken and tamed for our ownership.

It's more expansive than that – defiant, even.

But you'll know it when you see it... or feel it... or find yourself swept clean off your feet by the tide of its arrival. And it is arriving. Relentless in its quiet rising, Goodness isn't waiting around for our recognition to do its work in the world. It's always creeping into unexpected places, taking us off guard and daring us to live in the adventure of its discovery.

The Good wife

Just the other day, I met a man; his thin leather skin was as wrinkled as the unpressed t-shirt draped over the chair where he sat in the mid-morning sun. This wasn't our first meeting, but he didn't remember that. His ninety-year-old mind was losing its grip on the snapshots of a well-lived life. "I spoke at your grandson's wedding," I said.

His eye glinted briefly in response. "Ah yes, I remember."

I could tell that he did, for a moment, and then he did not. Disappearing behind his wide-brimmed hat, he drifted off to some distant place within himself. I stood there, unsure of what to feel. I had heard of him from my friend, his grandson, who I was visiting that day. In the stories he was iconic. His sage wisdom and faithful care shaped my friend in meaningful ways. Now, he just seemed tired. Worn down, like a frayed rope, to a few fragile strands.

Suddenly, she arrived, waddling her way toward us like a luminescent penguin.

Her skin, like his, was stretched loose and sun stained. Her hair, wild and brittle, was more like hay than a Pantene commercial. You could almost hear her creaking joints and feel her aching bones. But none of that was what you noticed first. Her soul, or something like it, seemed to run out before her, like a praise singer preparing the way for royalty. The closer she came, the more the settling sadness lifted, like the morning sun burning clean the hovering mist of winter.

Joy is what it felt like. A spark in her eyes. A smirk on her face. Light, almost pouring out of her even as the weight of the day pressed down her drooping shoulders. She was a walking contradiction before she spoke a single word. Something eternal was breaking through in bursts from the fading tent that was her ageing frame.[21]

This was his wife.

"Good morning," she beamed with a cheeky smile.
"Good morning," I responded with a smile that hers pulled out of me.
"Are you staying here?" she asked.
"I'm just visiting," I said.

She nodded approvingly and turned her attention to her husband. Like me, he sensed her presence. It called him back from distant places. Emerging from the shadow of that wide-brimmed hat, he lifted his gaze to meet hers. They just looked at each other for a moment. Their gentle smiles reminded me of home. I wondered what silent words they shared in that space between breaths. Whatever was said, it felt holy. The deep lines that cracked seams across their faces testified to grief, joy, and a lifetime of friendship.

It awakened something in me.

Like a child standing on tiptoe, I could feel myself stretching to get a better view of the unexpected wonder climbing through the pain of their breaking.

None of us relish ageing. There is nothing romantic about the unwelcome intrusion of death. And yet, there amidst the undeniable weight of it all, something raised a whisper from their love that held more substance and hope than the darkness of a thousand shadows.

I don't know what it was exactly, but I know that it was Good.

Hall of fame

I hope you've had those moments. I hope you've found yourself taken aback at the standing ovation pulled out of you by the unannounced arrival of Goodness. It's a wonderful thing to be sideswiped by something so pure. It is why we are moved to take pictures or write stories when it happens.

We want to capture the moment like a lifeline for when we're tripping over the tied laces of busy days.

It's why we frame the names of the brave ones on polished plaques in our collective mind. A hall of fame where Mother Teresa, Martin Luther King Junior, Nelson Mandela, Desmond Tutu, Rosa Parks, Dorothy Day, and Corrie Ten Boom, to name a few, are locked up and guarded from the darkness. As if by instinct, we immortalise our heroes, revealing with every portrait and plaque how deeply we long for the Goodness they embodied to be our own.

The craving

After viral voices fade
And tycoon gold gives in to the grave
And boulevards of star-struck-fame
Are trodden vague by squeaking sneakers.

Their names remain.

Iconised, no doubt,
Stuffed full to bursting seams
With aspirations and dreams
Of all we hoped we'd be if not for the weight of our living.

But honest.

Our hearts displayed in their gaze
Like moth to flame,
That iridescent craving refusing to be tamed
By the cynic.

Goodness.

Stretching far desperate limbs to reach its own reflection.
Shaking free debris and dust
From the dim space it was left in,
Forgotten but not gone.

Still breathing, and hopeful, and strong.

Ready for the finding

It's as if our heroes haunt us. Try as we may, they just won't let us give up on our potential. And yet, ironically, they often stop us from embracing it as well.

You see, the challenge with plaques and portraits is that they're not real.

The names and faces set high on the pedestals of our admiration grow taller than those they belonged to and end up putting Goodness beyond the reach of ordinary mortals.

"I'm no Mother Teresa," we say. To which, Mother Teresa cries from the place beyond the grave: "Neither am I!"

None of the brave ones were as shiny as the statues we polish in their honour.

Teresa had bad days like the rest of us. Nelson woke to morning breath, and Desmond may have splurged on two-ply toilet paper. All saints wear scars up close, and the pursuit of perfection (the kind born in the same story that makes Botox big business and sells self-help books on 'seven steps to your greatness') keeps us so busy spinning hamster wheels that we miss the simplicity of Goodness in the pursuit of something more impressive.

In *The Old Story* – the one exploding through the keyhole – the Humanity that Truth calls Good is not fashioned from gold, it's formed from dirt. In that story, we're not diminished by our struggles and sufferings – quite the opposite. Our wounds, it turns out, are precisely where the light shines through.[22]

Weakness is the home of our strength.[23] That story calls us jars of clay, pre-loaded with luminescence just waiting to leak light through all the places now shrouded in the shadow of our shame.[24]

***The Old Story* insists that you, with all your failures and flaws, are not beyond the grasp of Goodness. None of us are.**

Look again at that hall of fame with honest eyes. See scraped knees and fragile frames. Wade knee-deep into complicated stories and find your reflection there. Get close enough to hear the laughter, singing, sighing, and whispered invitations spoken by those who wipe tears from wrinkled faces.

They're like witnesses in some great cloud of ordinary people insisting that,[25] despite evidence to the contrary, our world is packed tight as a treasure chest with Goodness ready for the finding.

What if we believed them?

Pause

Sideswipe

Have you ever noticed how two people can be in the same situation and experience it differently? One person might only see the bad in a moment, while another is able to see the good. Part of this is about personality (optimists as opposed to critics) but part of it is about how our brains work. You might imagine our brains like a collection of pathways. The more we repeat certain thoughts or give our attention to certain things, the more defined certain pathways become. Our thoughts typically prefer the route of least resistance and so choose pathways that are well-defined over those that are overgrown. This is what we mean when we talk about habits.

Some of us have developed a habit of missing Goodness.

Our thoughts run down well-worn paths of negativity that we have developed over time. Thankfully, our brains can change. We can build new pathways by giving our attention to new things over an extended period. Practising gratitude is one of the ways we can make a pathway, and build a habit of seeing Goodness in our lives.

- For the next week, before you go to sleep at night, take 5 minutes to reflect on your day.
- As you do, write down at least three things that you are grateful for from the day. This might be anything from a good cup of coffee in the morning to a moment of kindness from a friend.
- At the end of the week take some time to read through your gratitude list. Pay attention to the emotions that stir in you as you do.
- Write some reflections on how practising gratitude has made you more aware of Goodness in your life.

Six: Beauty

A kind of purple hue

"Beauty," that's what we call the soaring sparks that light the night where Truth and Goodness collide. It's what we feel when symphonies stir melodies so haunting that they pull gasps from our guts and make us ache in our bones. It's what holds our eyes wide open when sunsets burn liquid glory on glass waters and call the day to silence. It takes hostages in galleries, dripping its thick presence down paintings on the wall.

Beauty is fragile, as delicate as snowflakes settling on the skin of giggling children carving angels into gathering powder.

It is strong, unmoved sometimes, even by death. It mixes light and shade into a kind of purple hue that's never quite the same colour. You might have seen it wash across the clasped hands of a faithful wife at the bedside of her dying husband, or in the wiped-clean eyes of a mother, now terminal, counting cards on the carpet with her unaware daughter.

I feel it when my arms stretch tight around my shoulders and squeeze. It reminds me of the last time I hugged my father. If I knew that all our hugs through all the years would find their end in that one, I'd still be standing on those steps and savouring the smell of him. It hurts, even now, to think of it, but I'd never want to forget.

Each tear that forms in his memory flows from a deep well that we dug in a lifetime of loving.

Selling sunsets

Beauty is not sentimental, cheap, or puffed up with positive thinking. Nothing so thin could bear its weight when it walks through the door. It is deeper, higher, and wider than that, calling us back from the puddle-like lives in which we splash with a hushed, confident voice.

Beauty does not fight for attention.[26]

And yet, for all the breath that it has stolen, it is profoundly useless sometimes. Unlike a hammer for the striking, a blade for the slicing, or an ice-cold Coke to quench your thirst, Beauty doesn't always have a reason for its being.

Sometimes, Beauty just is.

That's why we miss it. We don't know what to do with things that can't be sold. Even sunsets are for sale these days. Except they're not. Every price tag hanging clumsily on a burning horizon robs the twilight of its mystery. Beauty retreats with every bid we make to buy it until whatever it is we're selling isn't a sunset anymore.

It's just self-tan sprayed on a sky full of pretence and anxious striving for control.

Losing control

That's where Beauty leads – beyond illusions of control. There, with Truth and Goodness, it stands patient and waiting on the path. The one that winds far beyond the fog into those wild places that have no use for maps and navigation apps. Where we're stripped clean of power and plunged neck-deep into vulnerable waters.

Like a baptism... or a washing machine. True Beauty overwhelms us when we choose it. Head beneath feet, it carries us away with every breath surrendered to its flow. We drown in its surging, washed wide awake into a single, sober, revelation.

We are not the main event.

The wave

One time, I caught a wave so big it right-sized me in a second. I was bobbing on the backline like a cork; my longboard smelt like fresh wax as the swell surged in set by set. The morning was straight out of the womb, still settling into the day unfolding before its amber light. It was cold – cold enough to make you breathe deeply and smile wide in the crisp exhilaration of the moment.

Seagulls carved ripples in the tides as they swooped low to meet them in their rising. It looked like fire dripping off the tips of their wings each time that they did. I turned my head to take in the sunrise and – not a word of a lie – a pod of dolphins raised their fins to cut the water closer than I could throw a stone.

I laughed so deeply, it felt like a prayer.

I guess I was grateful... pensive... alive. Of course, it doesn't stay a picture postcard when you're trying to ride the ocean. At some point, the time comes to paddle. You look back, lie flat, and pull yourself across the water stroke by tiring stroke. This is what I did.

The swell was fast approaching. I spotted a forming heap in the deep that felt like mine for the taking so I started to paddle. Four strokes in, I looked again. The modest heap was now a mountain. The kind they call a rogue. It rushed up behind me without warning or mercy and lifted me like a geyser. Blood drained fast from my face as ocean spray stung my skin in the wind now whistling through my ears.

Fear came clamouring – a wave of its own, it pried control from my white-knuckled fingers. Something like instinct triggered as fast as falling dominos. Quick-hands-fast-feet. I was standing and sliding at breakneck speed down the churning face of Everest... for a second... until a force that felt like a landmine ripped me off balance and crumpled me like paper. Water fell heavy as a hammer and wrapped tight around my foetal frame; I was a tumbling stone churning in power desperately waiting to breathe. Gravity was a stranger there. Those wild waters had no reverence for earth or sky; all was writhing chaos –

until the light.

Blinding, bright salvation met me as I burst above the surface and sucked in more air than I could use in a lifetime. I swam out of the wash, hobbled over rocks, and found my waiting board on the beach. Sinking down beside it, I stared out at the place that could have been my grave. It was calmer now. Gentle waves were riding tides and lapping at my feet. I just sat there, feeling smaller than the grains of sand between my toes, in my ears, and up my nose.

"This all goes on without me," I thought.

"These oceans have carved back the earth since the first dawning day. They'll keep pounding its shores till the last gathering night. And all the while, people like me throughout the generations will find space, for a moment, to join them."

I smiled, grateful for the grace that allowed my intrusion and the mercy that left me alive.

It was all so... Beautiful.

Naked

Yes, Beauty can be found resting gently on the mantelpiece where it washes lilies bright with colour. It frames faces with a symmetry that turns them into muse. It drapes elegant lines down flowing gowns with a grace that moves like air on skin. Beauty is there in all the usual places. It is not less than catwalks and cologne, it's simply so much more.

Beauty is a reckoning.

In its purest form, it sweeps us clean off our pole position podium and straight into a story of which we are not the centre. It strips us naked there, as naked as we were in the garden of our first forming.[27] Naked enough to open like a womb in all our disarmed wonder to the gift of becoming ourselves.

Beauty, when we let it, can make us Human.

Pause

Get naked

Sometimes we just need to take it in. To 'get naked' in the path of oncoming beauty and let it have its way without trying to own it, analyse it or control it. That is precisely what I'm inviting you to do now.

- For the next week, find at least one moment each day to place yourself in the path of oncoming Beauty.[28] This might look like lying outside and staring at the stars before you go to bed, waking up early to make a good cup of coffee and appreciate the sunrise, or taking ten minutes to sit in your comfiest chair and listen to music that draws a deep sigh from your chest. You can get as creative as you like with this.

- Resist the temptation to analyse your experience in the moment. Simply allow yourself to be caught up in Beauty.

- At the end of the week, take some time to reflect.

- What did you learn about your need for Beauty from this exercise? You might want to write your thoughts down.

- How might you make more room for Beauty in your life going forward? Again, it might be helpful to write your thoughts down.

Seven: Him

Paper castles

How are we doing? I know, it's been a roller-coaster ride so far. To be fair, I did tell you that this question was a fire hazard. We're only three steps down our path to being Human and, if you're paying attention, you can already hear flames licking at the door of the paper castle stories we've been living in till now.[29]

It's as if their flimsy frames catch fire in the bright light of what's real.

Of course, not everyone hears that as good news. Many of us quite like our paper castle kingdoms; they may be made of paper, but they're kingdoms nonetheless. So, when the life we thought we wanted threatens the one we've come to know, we can surprise ourselves with how quickly we go running for the sprinklers to put out the flames.

A word of advice, if I may, "Don't do it!"

"Don't fight the flames of your deliverance. Let them burn."

And, while you're out there in the raging, let the glimpses we've seen of Beauty, Goodness, and Truth be enough to wash you wide awake, into a holy longing for the kind of life you had nearly forgotten was possible. A life that feels as full as the story it is born in.

The one we spied through the keyhole.

I imagine us climbing the shoulders of that story now, inching taller on the heights of its substance in defiance of those flames that rise higher as we do. Yes, our paper walls are burning, but I don't see us trembling with fear. We're not running for water or turning on taps to point a hose at the windows now melting in the heat.

Instead, we're wide-eyed and waiting with buckets full of fuel.

You see, much to my surprise and in ways I can't explain, I'm slowly starting to believe that just beyond the burning down of all the worlds we've made is a rebirth into the world that we were made for.

In other words, it's precisely in our dying that we're born.

Vessels

We are Human.
We know that now.
Not just the mind-numbed masses jostling for power.

Not fodder for the wars of men
Not pouring out our hours
Like an offering on altars to the idols all around us.

We are the image of another.
Shaped from earth by Holy hands,
Formed as vessels for the filling
Painted artwork on a canvas.

Made for heaven.
Even as we tread the dirt.
Leaking life with every footstep,
Bleeding balm to heal the hurt.

And none of this is of our own.
We're not the main event.
Our radiance to magnify The Life that swallows death.

Yes!
We are Human.

The liar

What a vision... that in our dying we might live into something as luminous as this! It's a hope so lofty that we'd be forgiven for the vertigo that flows from its speaking. Especially if it's true. If there is more to this than poetry and stories, if these words are calling a witness in our chest to stand tall in recognition of what's real, well then, we're at a threshold, my friends. Decisions are waiting to be made.

Save the paper castles or surrender to the flames. Some of us have heard enough. We're braced and ready for the burning, that is until the phone pings a loud headline from the morning.

"Some stranger sent a bullet through the windshield
of the lady down the street.
He took a cheap Armani knockoff.
She didn't make it."

With that, a flood of doubt rips loose the ground forming beneath us. Another headline pings: "Rockets level buildings, burying families alive."

We're spinning now, catching glimpses of ourselves in the mirror as we do. Every wayward inclination, every dark and sinister thought, every lingering shadow of shame rushes forward to accuse us: "How foolish! How naïve to follow longings like they're real! Humanity isn't Beautiful, Good, or yearning for Truth. It's lost in the dark. Come to think of it, so are you."

Hope springs a leak and drains fast through holes in our feet. Suddenly we're scrambling for hoses and frantically dousing flames. We're fighting to contain the damage to the paper walls that we were seconds away from leaving.

Retreat is what they call it.

Breathless and shaken, we collapse on a crate in some smouldering corner. Disappointment settles thicker than the ash now slowly falling to the ground; our faith falls with it. We're pushed back from the belief that anything as grand as being Human is possible, and we settle into the lesser stories where hope once found us. If any of that sounds familiar, please know you're not alone. Becoming Human isn't easy. If it were, everyone would do it.

You see, the thing with paper castles is they have a paper king.

He's a liar. In the beginning, he tempted the first of us to trade glory for a midday snack. He's been lying ever since with intricate deception made to overfeed our ego and blind us to our design. So, when his paper walls start burning (flimsy as they are in the heat of rising light) he doesn't just sit back and let it slide, he puts up a fight. Unfortunately, he's not just good at lying, he's the father of lies.[30] In collusion with the sickness we collected from our ancient falling, and the broken world we're in that's quietly shaping us all, he starts swinging.[31]

We're overwhelmed by the onslaught. Faith gets punched clean out of our lungs as we crumble to the mat, which sadly is where many of us stay. But here's the thing. The fight is not over till the bell rings. Contrary to all his slick deception, darkness doesn't get the final word. All the evil wrecking homes across nations, and all the shame, fear, and failure lurking just beneath our skin, none of it needs to be a death sentence. I'm begging you to listen. We don't need to make his paper walls our home.

We just need to recognise that we can't become Human alone.

Help

To quote an ancient sage: "The good life belongs to the needy"[32] which, I know, is borderline offensive in our society of strength. A place where might (most often) makes right, and no one is selling tickets to a TED talk on how to be weak.

And yet, those of us who've been humbled under the dismantling effects of our destructive tendencies know full well that weak is precisely what we are. Constant collisions with the low ceiling of your capacity are a quick cure for grandiose illusions of sufficiency. Of course, there is much we can do. History speaks of our resourcefulness, but it also assures us of our limits. For all we have achieved, the tragic cycles of our past and the slippery slopes that fill our present are a sobering reminder of our fragilities.

The Humanity we long for is – it would seem – firmly planted in the ground beyond our reach.

We need help. Not the kind of help that trickles down in handouts from distant places of power, or slides across screens in "Six Steps for Thriving" from talking heads on reels.

No, we need more than that. We need help that heals, help that bleeds, help with bruised palms and grazed knees that are well acquainted with each thistle and weed of our being.[33] Help that's walked the dead-end streets of our sin-stained stories and burst through barred doors into the bright day of full life living.

We need help that's made a way we can walk in.

Well-intentioned, as it may be, the help we need won't come from those of us still stumbling around in our own shadows – not entirely. The blind don't lead the blind to freedom.[34]

What we need is help that can see.

So, if – like me – you're convinced about your weakness and persuaded of your need, then lean in as I tell you one more story. Imagine with me.

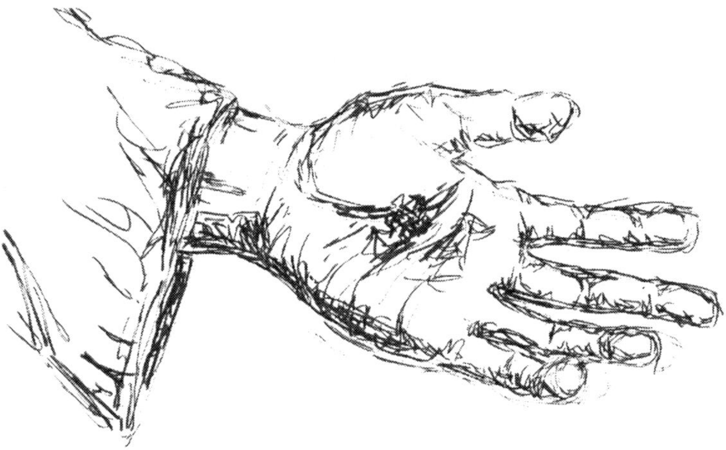

The temple[35]

It's dark out; the world is draped silver and blue by the moon. Stillness gently parts like water with each sand-crunching step you take up the hill you're slowly climbing. Now and then some sleeping thing startles awake with your passing and rustles into the darkness for safety. It's lonely, and you're thirsty, but you heard that he was here.

Him. Life seemed simpler before him.

Not better. Not even good. Just simpler. You laugh quietly to yourself at the absurdity of it all. Not long ago you had no idea who he was and now you're climbing a mountain near midnight to find him.

It's the temple that did it. Not just the temple of course. Other things are pushing you up this hill. Rumour has it, that he spoke sight into a blind man's eyes,[36] and that he sits easy over meals with people who don't usually find themselves at dinner parties (At least not the respectable kind).[37]

As you're walking, you remember the commotion of his arrival a few days earlier.

Crowds crammed the sidewalk filling the air with loud words about a king and the floor with palm leaves like a red carpet. You remember how he slowly ambled uphill toward the temple, sitting sideways on a donkey... a donkey! Some king, you thought at that moment. Where was the stallion, where were the soldiers, where was the trumpet sound? He didn't look like any king you had ever seen.

Come to think of it, he didn't look like very much at all.

That's when you left to get on with the day. You had seen his kind before, one more mad man selling stories to the desperate about freedom. If only freedom were coming. It never came. All there was, was this: money to lend, pigeons to buy, and sacrifices to make to a God who didn't seem to be paying much attention to the smoke that rose in His honour.

That's when it happened.

Right in the thick of one more day at the temple, just as a vendor reached out his calloused hand to drop two coins into your own, a voice rolled over the humming masses like thunder.

All the haggling and hustling quickly fell to silence. The cooing of pigeons and bleating of sheep echoed awkwardly in the space. The thundering voice came rolling again. You stretched to see what was going on. It was him, the donkey-riding stranger. Except it wasn't him. He looked different somehow. Was he taller now and almost glowing? Memories can be tricky like that. Whatever it was, you remember him having your attention.

"MY FATHER! HOUSE OF PRAYER! CRIMINALS!"

You couldn't hear every word, it was a big space filled with people from all over the region, but you got the gist. Suddenly, he raised a whip and cracked the air like lightning. CRACK! People cowered low in shock. Another lightning strike, CRACK! Panic erupted into chaos as people scrambled in every direction. Before you knew it, sheep were charging past your feet. One almost rammed you to the ground. Pigeons, freed from their cages, filled the air. Money splashed like spilt water all over the floor in loud clatterings as this madman rushed straight past you. He flipped table after table after table. With each one, it felt as if he were flipping your whole life.

That's why you're here on this mountain.

You need to meet him. You need to know if he is the king they say he is. You desperately need a king. When you asked around town, they told you that he often came up here to pray. Not that you know where here is. They just pointed to a path and told you to follow it. You did. Now you've been walking for almost an hour and are beginning to wonder if you're lost. As you round a corner, your thoughts are interrupted. Not more than ten meters ahead, the path levels out into a garden. Olive trees are scattered all around. They're not very tall, but they are thick, almost making a low canopy that filters moonlight into dappled pools of blue and silver on the floor. "This must be the place," you whisper; The Oil Press is what they called it.[38]

The garden

You slow your pace, careful not to make too much noise. You saw him travelling with others that day at the temple. If they had followed him up here, they wouldn't be welcoming some stranger looking for their leader at midnight. Just to be safe, you step off the path and carefully start creeping through shrubs and trees for cover. You're hunched over now, gently placing one foot in front of the other and breathing quietly as you do.

A low hum to your left stops you dead in your tracks. Peering through silver-washed leaves and staying hunched low to the cold ground, you see them. Three men are leaning up against a tree. They're sleeping. One of them is snoring gently. None of them look comfortable. Come to think of it, none of them look peaceful either. The air feels heavier here somehow, and theirs like the kind of sleep you run to when you're trying to numb the pain of living.[39]

Another sound breaks the darkness to your right.

A mumbling – you can't quite see where it's coming from. With gentle steps, you creep closer until the trees thin and the branches part into a clearing. There on the floor, hunched up like a trembling boulder, is a man. He's alone, not physically alone – his friends are nearby asleep against a tree, it's more than that, he feels lonely. It's like he's lost in some other place beyond this garden, a place you couldn't get to if you tried.

You keep watching. He keeps trembling and swaying on the ground, mumbling as he does. You try to hear what he's saying, "Father... Father... Father!"

Again and again, whispered out between sobs and sighs, he keeps... praying. Yes, that's what he's doing, he's praying. The strained whispers keep coming, "Father..."

Flashbacks of the temple, of the madman with the whip. That echoing phrase: "MY FATHER'S HOUSE!" It hits you.

This is Him!

The one you came here for. You lean forward ready for an awkward introduction. But you're interrupted mid-stride by a sudden, violent writhing from the trembling stone of a man before you. Rising from his hunched-over state, he rips his head from his hands and throws it back toward the heavens. You're startled and stumble backwards. Did you trip over your own feet or was it the grief (now flooding out of him in waves) that sent you flying? Either way, you are flat on your back and overwhelmed. In some way you can't explain, a deep pain within him has now broken its banks and is rushing out over the whole garden in wave after tangible wave.

Everything is affected.

The silver blue moonlight drains of colour leaving only sickly pools of dappled grey scattered thin across the floor. The leaves, dancing elegantly in the soft breeze just moments ago, now hang limp and wilted on their stems. And you, now reeling with shock, can feel a terrible, ominous weight pressing down on your chest.

It slowly squeezes the life out of you like a python cracking ribs with every tightening coil of its body. Fear, dread, shame, regret, and every other awful thing collected over a lifetime and buried in the places you've tried hard to forget, come surging forward in an overwhelming storm of emotion. Tears flood your searching eyes. Your heart feels close to collapsing under the weight of it all. You want it to stop. You need it to stop. You gather the wisps of breath still left in the recesses of your chest and try to call for help. Nothing, no sound, only a stifling, suffocating void. His scream invades your panicking mind like a foghorn.

"FATHER, PLEASE!"

You're able to lift your head enough to get a glimpse of his face. Agony hangs thick on every inch of it. Tears pour in rivers from his puffed-up eyes and... is that blood dripping like sweat from his brow? What on earth, in heaven, or lurking in the darkest parts of hell could wring a man out like a rag?

What weight of grief could crush a man to bleeding?

Another part of your heart caves in under the mounting pressure of his suffering. It's drowning you and everything else with its force. His murmuring prayers start building again, from whispers to guttural groans.

The python around your chest gets tighter with each of his heaving sighs. Your head falls back as you stare desperately at the sky. You're breathing in sips now, paralysed beneath the unbearable load that keeps building. Your vision blurs and the sound of the night slowly gives way to ringing in your ears. Heavier, heavier, heavier... your consciousness is fading. Just as all is about to go black, another scream cuts through the dark and pulls you back from the abyss.

"FATHER, PLEASE!"

It stops. Everything stops. The python-like pressure that was crushing your chest slowly unwraps itself and slips back into whatever dark place it came from. The surging waters of pain suddenly pause and slowly recede. The moonlight moves from grey to pale blue silver and the leaves resume their gentle dance in the breeze. You push yourself up off the floor. Blood runs back to your hands and feet as you do.

He is still there. He's hunched over like a boulder again, head in hands and mumbling his prayers. But the trembling has stopped. In this place, soaked thick as mud with the desperate dark of grief just moments ago, something else is steadily rising.

It feels like comfort.

Yes... comfort, the kind that calls strength out of weakness.[40] It's washing over him now just as grief had done before. It's pouring out in torrents and overflowing to you. With every wave, you're reminded of the morning sun that gently warms your skin in the cold of winter, and the strong arms of your parents that held you together as a child.

You can feel breath returning to your lungs as you sit there in the dirt. You imagine something similar must be happening to him. He's as still as a stone and quietly mumbling prayers.
This goes on for a while; you don't know how long. It feels like neither an age nor an instant, but eventually, the waves slow and start to recede as if someone, somewhere, is turning off a tap.

The comfort gives way to silence.

No mumbling prayers. No trembling, swaying groans. Even the leaves hang still to make way for the blanket now settling over him, and you, and everything in the garden. It isn't regular silence. Something more is happening now. This feels... final.

It's like the full stop at the end of the last word in a long letter. There is nothing left to say, only whatever comes next.

It is, at that moment, as if the sky itself leans low as dirt to join with everything in all the world and pay homage.

This must be what they mean by 'holy'.

He starts unfolding, slowly at first and then more steadily. Without a word, he rises to his feet. The ground beneath him is wet. It reminds you of dew that settles damply in the morning. You shift further back into the shadows in some combination of fear, compassion, and awe. You don't think that he has seen you. It's better that way. You're not sure you should have been here, intruding on something as sacred as this. But you were. You saw what you saw, and felt what you felt, and everything is different now.

You don't know why exactly, you just know that it is.

He dusts himself off with slow, weary swipes. He drags a sleeve across his forehead; sweat, dirt, and blood are caked thick on his skin. With both hands he wipes clean the tear stains trailing down his face and into his scruffy beard. Dragging in a deep, heavy sigh, he straightens his back and steals one more glance at the sky.

There's fire in his eyes.

Some strange mixture of ferocity and sadness. He turns toward those sleeping men propped up against a tree and slowly walks away. You don't follow him; you couldn't if you tried. You just sit there in the silver-blue moonlight, staring into nothing and trying to make sense of what just happened.

Pause

Take it in

Familiarity can rob us of awe. Some of the most wonderful things in existence have been stripped of their glory by the jaded eyes of our familiarity. This is certainly true of Jesus. I can't even type His name without crashing into the wall of assumptions that each of us carries about Him. Somehow, we need to find a way over that wall if we hope to see Him – or anything else for that matter – clearly. Imagination can help us with this. It has a way of riding the tide of story and emotion past the dragons of religion and the guardians of the mind into the fertile soil of the heart.[41] I'm hoping you'll take a risk with me, regardless of what you do or don't believe, and spend some time imagining this moment in the garden again.

- Start by settling into silence. Deep breaths in, deep breathes out, for about a minute.

- When you are ready, re-read the story of the garden, but don't just read it. Imagine it. Plant your feet firmly in the earth as you walk through it, notice the smells of the olive trees as you breathe it in, feel the cool breeze, and hear the groans from the praying man hunched up in the moonlight. Let the story stir emotions that don't need to be qualified by your critical mind.

- When you are done, take a moment to simply sit with your emotions. As they settle and swirl in you, try to name at least one of them. *'That made me feel...'*

- Is there an invitation beneath that emotion (Something you might explore further or do in response to what you are feeling)? It might be a good idea to write this down.

Eight: Knowing

The wild ground of encounter

I don't know what you think about Jesus. To be honest, that's not my main concern, at least not right now. Opinion abounds when it comes to this traveller from Nazareth whose influence saturates history like water soaking a sponge.

Experience is far rarer.

Imagine the absurdity of students in the garden that night. A group of people clutching pens and scribbling notes to publish papers in the morning for a grade. All the while Jesus, a person, writhes in agony on the floor under the crushing weight of our collective darkness and the terrible awareness of his impending torture.

Do surveys in the queue to the gas chambers of Auschwitz seem fitting to you? Do we quench the flames of lovers at the height of their passion to deliver a lecture on romance?

Some things, the deepest things perhaps,
are more to be known than they are to be known about.

Neither the awful dark of crippling grief nor the euphoric light of rapturous joy are honoured in their arrival by the cold distance of analyses and assessment. It's why the truest things about us – our longings – invite us to descend from the heights of the mind into the depths of the heart.[42]

That chasmic voyage of eighteen inches
that makes alpinists of us all.

It is why Truth is a base beat humming in the room next door, shaking loose our floorboards and daring us to dance. It's why Goodness is a side swipe, knocking us off balance in those unexpected moments that hum with the frequency of heaven, and it is why Beauty is a reckoning, a tidal wave of wonder that rips us into the surging current of a story far greater than our own.

It's why Jesus (the man we met in the garden) is not first a theory, religion, or theological tome, but a person. Not just to be known about but waiting to be known.

Faith, it turns out, is better built on the wild ground of encounter than in the heady musings of men.[43]

Lessons on learning to breathe.

At this point, let me name the elephant that's crept in through the back door and is standing in the middle of the room. I'm sure, to some, it feels like we took a left turn at the garden. Our conversation has been meaningful, honest, and real. We've been wading through tears, curled up in laughter, sighing deep sighs, and wiping our eyes in the common recognition of all that it means to be Human.

Now we're talking about Jesus.

How did we shift from relatable things, like dishes and ice cream, to the far-flung places of religion? That dusty antique in some back alley pawn shop, forgotten by all except the most serious of collectors.

What an illuminating question!

How indeed. How did we strip the sacred from the kitchen sink and peel glory off the bathroom walls like fading paint? Why have we tried to box up heaven and lock it tight under the shadow of a steeple, singing songs to the god of the professionals who grants the desperate an audience each Sunday before sending them back to their lives? Not that there's anything wrong with Sundays, steeples, or songs. They're as good a place as any to meet God, but so are gardens, office blocks, and checkout queues at grocery stores that rival the Great Wall of China in their torturous length.

Are we hung up on stories of a distant creator? Is God as still as a statue in our imagination, waiting immovable behind rituals and offerings that break the backs of those who drag them uphill to some temple? Let me be clear,

"Jesus utterly obliterates these paradigms."

Whatever space He left to tread the dirt of earth is surely the home of the anti-god. A God so utterly uninterested in being god[44] that He drained Himself empty of deity, embraced the form of flesh and walked our world as a servant.[45]

The God whose final exhalation ripped wide a temple curtain (one we seem intent on repairing) to shatter a box holding heaven and pour it out into the streets.[46]

The God who comes to us as Human.

More human than we're comfortable with, if we're honest. We like our gods dressed up in decorum. Jesus erupts from a womb dripping with placenta. He feasts at tables with reprobates, swigging wine and tearing bread to mop up olive oil from his plate. He rages with fierce impropriety at the injustices we've numbed ourselves to for the sake of staying civil. He weeps with naked vulnerability under the pressing weight of grief. He lives like a whirlwind in wild surrender to a life beyond our own. He dies – not in some sanitary way that makes for good art to hang in our chapels, but brutally. He dies with a suffering that would turn our stomachs and twist our heads at the sight of it.

He is, in ways that stretch the word to bursting like an overfilled balloon, so utterly Human.

Of course, He's also more than that. We can still hear echoes bouncing off the walls of an empty tomb just outside Jerusalem, but let's not get ahead of ourselves. Wisdom builds a bridge before it tries to break a barrier. For now, it's important to acknowledge that any sense of irrelevance at the mention of Jesus in considering our humanity, is the product of unfortunate misperception at best and intentional deception at worst.

Jesus breaks the mould of peripheral religiosity.

Yes, you'll find Him in a pew if that's your place of preference, but you're just as likely to meet Him in a grimy bar on Friday night. He's the anti-god, remember? He's diving into dumpsters while other gods are posing under flashlights on some celestial red carpet.

He comes to us disguised as our life, as integral to the work of being Human as lessons on learning to breathe.[47] We haven't hijacked a compelling conversation with irrelevant god-talk in speaking about Jesus here.[48] Far from it. Jesus is precisely where any honest conversation on Humanity leads.

The exploration of our deepest longings propels us into an inevitable collision with the one who embodies them all.

Bearing witness

So, as we fasten our safety belts, lift our seats to the upright position, and prepare to land this plane, let's make sure the proposition before us is clear. This is not a call to get religion. There is no dotted line to sign, nor 'Ts and Cs' to comb through in the fine print.

This is a call to get honest.

Honest about what? About the ache. Honest about our yearning for more than we've found on our screens or been able to build with our own hands. As much as we try to deny it, when we stop long enough to pay attention, we find that we're crammed full of longings – deep, primal invitations that have been sliding through the mail slot in the front door of our lives ever since we were born. They're waiting there, piled high on the floor and ready for the journey. A journey that winds its way deep into the heart and straight off a cliff.

That's right... a cliff.

Much to our surprise, the journey into strength is first a journey into weakness. It is a humbling confrontation with the soul sickness of sin and an awakening to a chasm that can't be crossed on foot. It is as we've said, "We cannot become Human alone, we need help," which, is only a challenge for those who hope to be Human. Some, sadly, do not. But for those who do, for those who would follow their longings to the end of the path, an inevitable trust fall is waiting. Our becoming (or unbecoming, depending on how you frame it) lies beyond a ledge that we cannot think ourselves over.

At some point, we either take a leap or set up camp on the familiar ground of control.

If you can feel sobriety settling in your gut like an anvil right now, you're in good company. These are weighty propositions with innumerable implications. Only madmen go hurtling off mountains without seriously considering the consequences. Not every risk can be mitigated and not every eventuality seen, but hesitation is a healthy sign of comprehension in these matters.[49] Take whatever time you need, just do me a favour while you're waiting –

come to the cross.

It's where they took Him when they found Him in the garden that night. It's where millions have waited in wonder before us, and where millions more will do the same long after we're gone. Come join them on that sacred soil. Bring your longings in one hand and the question that started all this in the other. Side-line cynicism, back-shelf pride, and press pause on every lofty preconception. Then, in the spacious curiosity of a wide-open soul, simply allow yourself to bear witness.

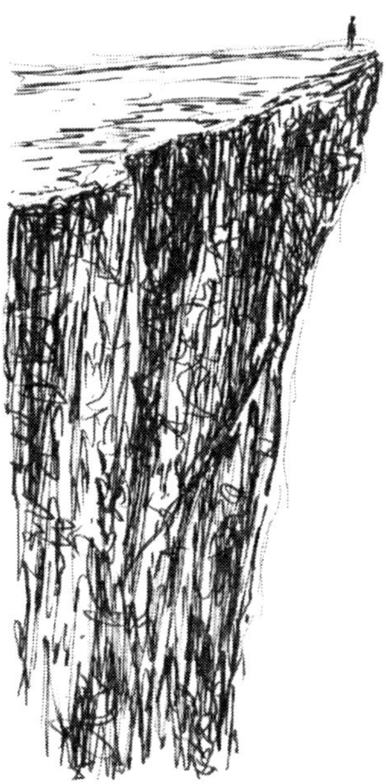

The Ambush

The dirt is stained a darker shade,
Soil soaked sodden by eyes that cry wild with unravelling.
Time is travelling slowly.

Like blood dripping thick down the crossbeam,
Holding hands pierced bone deep and deeper,
Nothing sweet here in the carnage.
A murder of the darkest kind.

Except His eyes.

His Eyes still shine defiantly.
Sun fails the sky
As cloud canvas wraps the day in darkness.

It's hardest to hear the groaning.

That audible pain
Ripping its way
Through silence that violence leaves
Hovering thick in the stunned souls who see it.

But do we?

See it?
See Him for who He is?
See clear enough
To read the sign above
The mocking crown pressed hard through splitting skin.
The word reads KING.

Take that in.

This is an ambush.
It's dressed down glory
With all heaven roaring
A Trojan horse straight into hell.

His final breath
A death blow to death
That no one saw coming.
It's stunning.

In ways that empty graves
As corpses raise chests
With fresh breaths of redemption,
Alive in the tension of words unleashed,
A closing speech that cracks the earth and tears temples to pieces.

IT IS FINISHED!

Collision

Go ahead and take a breath.

There's wonder in those words isn't there? It's not just about the cross. History is littered with those. It's about Him. When we see Him, not through the lens of Sunday school stories but in the bloody glory of a laid-down life,[50] we find ourselves still and undone. It's visceral. Some kind of soul-deep awakening not easily taped up in theory. I don't know what to call it, that feeling in my chest when I rest in the wake of it all.

I just know that it is True, Good, and Beautiful.

It's not just True in the historical sense. Although there is that. The weight of the evidence for this man and this moment is gravitational in force; it welcomes interrogation with arms wide as nails can stretch them and has been known to drag even the most reluctant of sceptics into a faith they had long tried to outrun.[51]

But It's Truer than that.

It's True in the way that bedrock is stable,[52] so True that it feels like safety. It is as if you could build a whole life on the firm ground of whatever substance is flooding every inch of His being. It feels like Truth is Him.[53]

A concentrated integrity more real and immovable than the wood on which He's bleeding, or the world He's dying in. So True, it makes you wonder if we're the ones doing the dying in our striving to snuff out the sun.

So True that it's Good.

Even there, in the scattered debris of hate and grief, clear eyes can see the Good still standing in irrepressible protest. Not the flimsy kind of good that smiles through squinted eyes while patting sitting dogs on the head.

Something far fiercer than that. The kind of Good that makes every altruistic aspiration and endeavour in all the worlds of women and men seem anaemic. Not just because a man hangs beaten and bleeding on a cross, but because a God-man does. That dumpster-diving deity who needs no appeasement or earning from those He's determined to love. This is the Goodness that waits without flinching for evil to finish fussing so it can get to work.

Bringing Beauty from wreckage.

Yes, Beauty. There may not be roses rising from the trampled dirt just yet. This is not a sight that infant eyes could easily process, but lingering onlookers testify with faces shrouded in awe, to the breath snatched from their chests by Beauty broken open and pouring fresh from His side.

There's a cleansing in those waters and courage in that heart enough to stir the stuff of sonnets. It's sacred and even as they lower limp limbs toward the waiting ground, it's burning back the darkness with a small but swelling flame that dares to whisper hope.

Yes, this is where our longings lead.

It's where they come from too. Beauty, Goodness, and Truth converge in a collision so holy that it ripples redemption through time like a stone thrown strongly into the waters of history.

Redemption that rises, wave after wave, to crash heavily into hearts stretched open by beholding.

Beholding that pulls us deep below the surface of our own lives to plant us firmly in the soil of encounter.

Encounter with The Man.[54] The one who, even now, holds out those same scarred hands that bled crimson on a cross and waits for us to trust Him.

The God wrestlers

If, like me, you find trust spluttering in fits and starts from the burgeoning streams of your searching heart, let me set your mind at ease.

It is precisely in that unexpected mingling of certainty and doubt that we find ourselves in the good company of the God wrestlers. Those searching saints who limp the earth as evidence of the fight they fought for the blessing of a new name.[55]

You're no apostate in your allergy to easy answers and half-truths. Wrestling isn't an illness. Wrestling is the tradition we're invited into. Throughout the generations, God has called His people to a trust that is more nuanced and compelling than we may at first have imagined, one that we might have to wrestle our way into. That's certainly been true for me.

The mystery and the builder

There is more mystery than clarity packed into the place I call my faith. My tight grip has slipped over the years, stretched thin in the tension of living. Once-firm convictions have gently moved aside in a necessary shedding of baggage on the narrowing pathway home.[56]

But, while some things fade into obscurity in all the cosmic decluttering, others resolve into sharp focus. With each decrease in the decibels of noise, they set, firm as concrete, and anchor those floating mists of mystery to the immovable earth of Truth. It's a wonderful paradox of being.

One of those things is Jesus.

He's not the man I first met so many years ago. He's undressed from all the preferences and perceptions I used to try and turn Him into me. But, surprisingly, considering the poor company I have been, He is still here. With each passing day of our friendship, He seems to take up more space in the living room of my soul. He's not anxious there, but He is active. Moving around those creaky floorboards and tidying up the place, He packs coffee cups away to make room on the dining room table. I'm glad He let me keep it. Not all the things that used to fill this space survived His eye for detail. There's a graveyard in the back garden filled with trinkets and trophies that didn't fit the aesthetic of the world He is building here.

He looks at me with a spark in His eye that I've come to recognise as the beginning of trouble. He has a flair for the dramatic, this Jesus. He pulls a fresh set of blueprints from His bag and rolls them out on the varnished wood where they slap open in their unveiling. My eyes scan the dark lines that build shapes all over the paper. It's a daunting proposition for sure. Much of it will be painful. But, gulping down a cocktail of anxiety and gratitude, I take a deep breath and prepare for the re-building.

While I was ready to make a little cabin out of me, He seems set on a palace.[57]

Follow me

There are many answers to our question of what it means to be Human. Every person with a podcast (and there are more of those than necessary) is slinging speech to preach their opinion on the subject. I'm one of them, I guess. So, let me say this:

"In all the mingled ambiguity of heartbreaks and hallelujahs that living has served me, I have found neither companion nor master as proficient in the lost art of being Human as Jesus."

The first of us fumbled the fullness of our image in the garden all those lifetimes ago. It shattered, and we shattered with it. One billion shards flung like fading stars into every corner of creation. Jesus, the hopeless restorer that He is, pulled every piece back together in the pattern of His life and invited us to follow Him.[58]

I don't know where we go from here. Probably back to that cliff and the inevitable trust fall that awaits us all in the new light of each morning. I just hope that even there, where firmament falls into faith, where paper walls flicker with flame and hurricanes rage, and dishes lie stacked in lukewarm water and we laugh, and cry, and choose to leave our lies behind and listen deeply to our longing souls. I hope that even there, we would hear His whispered invitation to follow Him home and whisper a few words of our own.

"I'm coming."

Pause

The trust fall

Persuasion is the work of salesmen, not simple writers like me. I'm much more interested in presentation. I hope to hold Jesus before you and trust that an honest glimpse of Him will be all the persuasion you need. With that in mind, I offer you this final practice.

- As we have done so many times before, settle into the silence. Deep breaths in and out for about a minute.
- When you're ready let all that you have just read about Jesus settle in you. Pay attention to what rises up in your mind.
- How have these ideas about who Jesus is either confirmed or reframed your perspective of Him? You might want to write your reflections down.
- Now, imagine Jesus in your mind's eye. Imagine Him walking toward you and slowly asking you a question. What does He ask you? You might want to write this down.
- Sit a while with that question and when you are ready, write down your response.

Notes

[1] The idea of a 'thin place' is popular in Celtic spirituality. It refers to those places in the world that, by virtue of prayer or grace or some combination of the two, seem sacred in a unique way. It feels as though the space between heaven and earth is "thinner" there somehow.

[2] Eugene Peterson. *The Jesus Way - A Conversation in Following Jesus, Loc 706* (2009). Hodder & Stoughton General Div.

[3] Matthew 13:1–23; 31–32, *New International Version* (1984). Colorado Springs, International Bible Society (All Biblical references are form the same source unless otherwise stated).

[4] Genesis 2:18.

[5] "We can be human only together, black and white" Evelyn Lau, *A look back at Desmond Tutu's greatest quotes, from kindness to forgiveness*, The National News, 26 December 2021, Accessed 20 June 2024. https://www.thenationalnews.com/arts-culture/books/2021/12/26/a-look-back-at-desmond-tutus-greatest-quotes-from-kindness-to-forgiveness/

[6] Matthew 17:20–21.

[7] Luke 18:15–17.

[8] Definition of 'Human', *Oxford English Dictionary* (2000). Oxford, England: Oxford University Press.

[9] Psalm 139:13–14.

[10] *Indlamu* is a war dance that serves as a touchstone for Zulu identity. Particularly as it pertains to Zulu culture untouched by the West. https://www.researchgate.net/publication/369334819_Indlamu_An_Image_of_Zulu_Upper-class_Culture_of_the_Past

[11] Ecclesiastes 3:11.

[12] John 10:10.

[13] Jordan Peterson, *Here's why the Bible is true...* (2011) Available at: https://www.youtube.com/watch?v=KriS6RNZTPU (Accessed: 20 June 2024).

[14] Genesis 1; 2.

[15] Genesis 1:26.

[16] Clive Staples Lewis, *Mere Christianity*. Hammersmith, London: HarperCollins Publishers.

[17] John 12:24

[18] Matthew 5:13–16.

[19] One of the Hebrew words for 'sin' is an archery term that means: 'to miss the mark'.

[20] Genesis 1:31.

[21] 2 Corinthians 4:16; 5:1.

[22] Switch Foot (2016) *Where the light shines through*. San Diego, CA.: Vanguard.

[23] 2 Corinthians 12:9–11.

[24] 2 Corinthians 4:7–9.

[25] Romans 12:1.

[26] The secret life of Walter Mitty (2013). United States: 20th Century Fox.

[27] Genesis 1.

[28] Curt Thompson, *"In The Path of Oncoming Beauty"*, October 11, 2023, in The Being Known Podcast, Podcast MP3 audio, 45:00. https://thebeingknownpodcast.podbean.com/e/bkp-s8e1

[29] Hebrews 12:29.

[30] John 8:44.

[31] John Mark Comer, *Live no lies: Recognize and resist the three enemies that sabotage your peace (2021)*. Colorado Springs, CO.: Waterbrook.

[32] Matthew 5:3.

[33] Isaiah 53:3.

[34] Matthew 15:14.

[35] John 2:13–22.

[36] John 9:1–7.

[37] Mark 2:15.

[38] Mark 14:32, The word Gethsemane, which is the name of the garden where Jesus prayed before His crucifixion, can be translated as to mean Oil Press.

[39] Luke 22:45.

[40] Luke 22:43.

[41] Clive Staples Lewis, 'Sometimes fairy stories may say best what's to be said' (1956) *The New York Times*. Available at: https://www.nytimes.com/1956/11/18/archives/sometimes-fairy-stories-may-say-best-whats-to-be-said.html (Accessed: 20 June 2024).

[42] Ruth Hayley Barton, *Sacred rhythms: Arranging our lives for spiritual transformation,* p. 24. (2022). Downers Grove, IL: IVP.

[43] 1 Corinthians 2–5.

[44] Pete Greig [personal communication].

[45] Philippians 2:5–8.

[46] Matthew 27:50–51.

[47] Frederick Buechner quoting Paula D'Arcy. Buechner, F. (1983) *Now and Then: A Memoir of Vocation.* Cambridge (Cambridgeshire): Harper and Row.

[48] Peterson, Eugene H. Peterson, *When Kingfishers Catch Fire: A Conversation on The Ways of God Formed by the Words of God* (2017). Waterbrook.

[49] John 15:13.

[50] Luke 14:28–33.

[51] "I gave in, and admitted that God was God, and knelt and prayed: perhaps, that night, the most dejected and reluctant convert in all of England." Clive Staples Lewis, *Surprised by Joy: The Shape of my early life* (2017). San Francisco: Harper One.

[52] Psalm 18:2.

[53] John 14:6.

[54] John 19:5.

[55] Genesis 32:22-–32. In this story, we see Jacob, a patriarch of both the Jewish and Christian traditions, wrestling with a mysterious man. Many theologians believe that this is a Christophany, a manifestation of Jesus before the incarnation. What is so interesting about this story is the wrestle. Jacob wrestles with God and in the process receives two things: A limp, and a new name. In response to his desire for a blessing, God renames Jacob, "Israel". This would go on to become the name of God's chosen people. Directly translated, 'Israel' means something like, one who wrestles with God. As those who are grafted into the family of Israel through the sacrifice of Jesus, you might say that we have inherited the tradition of the God wrestlers.

[56] Matthew 7:13-14

[57] Lewis, Mere Christianity.

[58] Matthew 4:19

References

Barton, R. H. (2022) *Sacred rhythms: Arranging our lives for spiritual transformation*, p. 24. Downers Grove, IL: IVP.

Buechner, F. (1983) *Now and then: A memoir of vocation.* Cambridge (Cambridgeshire): Harper and Row.

Comer, J. M. (2021) *Live no lies: Recognize and resist the three enemies that sabotage your peace.* Colorado Springs, CO.: WaterBrook, an imprint of Random House, a division of Penguin Random House LLC.

Lewis, C. S. (2002) *Mere Christianity*. Hammersmith, London: Harpercollins Publishers.

Lewis, C. S. (1956) 'Sometimes fairy stories may say best what's to be said' The New York Times, 18 November. Available at: https://www.nytimes.com/1956/11/18/archives/sometimes-fairy-stories-may-say-best-whats-to-be-said.html (Accessed: 20 June 2024).

Lewis, C. S. (2017) *Surprised by joy: The shape of my early life.* San Francisco: HarperOne.

Oxford English Dictionary (2000) 'Human'. Oxford, England: Oxford University Press.

Peterson, E. H. (2017) *As kingfishers catch fire: A conversation on the ways of God formed by the words of God*. Colorado Springs, CO.: Waterbrook Press.

Peterson, E.H. (2009) *The Jesus Way - A Conversation in Following Jesus.* Hodder & Stoughton General Div.

Peterson, J. (2022) Here's why the Bible is true... Available at: https://www.youtube.com/watch?v=KriS6RNZTPU (Accessed 20 June 2024).

The Holy Bible. New International Version (1984) Colorado Springs, CO.: International Bible Society.

The secret life of Walter Mitty (2013) Directed by B. Stiller. USA: 20th Century Fox.

Thompson, C. "*In The Path of Oncoming Beauty*". The Being Known Podcast, October 11, 2023. Podcast MP3 audio, 45:00. https://thebeingknownpodcast.podbean.com/e/bkp-s8e1

Switch Foot (2016) *Where the light shines through*. San Diego, CA.: Vanguard.

20250120